MW00682896

BUSINESS CARDS
TO
BUSINESS
RELATIONSHIPS

Building the
Ultimate Network

ALLISON GRAHAM

Dedication

To my brother Tim, who taught me to dream big, persevere and believe in the impossible.

To my loving mom, Barb, who taught me it's nice to be important, but it's more important to be nice.

And to my dad, Robert James Graham (1944-2005), my best friend and sounding board for the first 30 years of my life. His wisdom continues to guide me. I wish he were here to share the journey.

Published by elevate Press
elevate Seminars + Strategic Development Inc.
305-611 Wonderland Road
London, Ontario
Canada N6H 5N7

First published in Canada in 2008
© elevate Press 2008

ISBN: 978-0-9810623-0-3

Graham, Allison
Business Cards to Business Relationships: Building the Ultimate Network
Allison Graham

All rights reserved. No part of this publication may be reproduced, stored in a
retrieval system or transmitted in any form or by any means, electronic, mechanical,
photocopying, recording or otherwise, without the prior written permission of either
the publisher or an entity authorized with restricted copying in Canada. This book
may not be lent, resold, hired out or otherwise disposed of by way of trade in any
form of binding or cover other than that in which it is published, without the prior
consent of the Publishers.

Contents

Section 3 The Fundamentals

Section 4 The Strategy

Acknowledgements

To properly acknowledge everyone who impacted my life so I could write this book would require a paperback of its own, arguably one worth writing. Everyone who makes up my ultimate network deserves some credit, large or small, for making this work a reality. To the people I have the privilege to know: thank you for letting me be a part of your lives.

As you can imagine, writing a book is a huge undertaking. After a year and a half of developing client programs and brainstorming ideas for this project, I knew that getting my thoughts on paper would require some focus and solitude. Thanks to the generosity of one couple, I was given the perfect chalet hideaway to do just that. I returned from that trip with cramps in my fingers from typing and a completed first draft.

Then came the editing phase – which has lasted for months. For as many late nights as I've spent mulling over the words in the pages that follow, my mom has spent the same. This book would never have come to fruition without her help and her encouragement.

To my several editors, thank you for taking time to read the book and give me feedback. Each of you offered a different, yet equally valuable, perspective for which I am grateful.

To my family and the many ultimate connectors who sparked my passion for proper networking and contributing to the community – thank you. Words can't express how grateful I am to have you in my life.

Thank you to Erin Rankin-Nash who invited me to the reception that unforgettable Saturday morning. She and her husband, David Nash, have been amazing friends ever since. Thank you for introducing me to Angus and Jean McKenzie. I can't imagine where I would be and what I would be doing if I hadn't met this couple who exemplify true community spirit. They invited me to join my first volunteer gala committee that began the domino effect for my career. Angus, it's a privilege to be one of your "recruits". Also, thank you to Bill and Linda Ross for their on-going encouragement. As ultimate connectors do, they continually give of themselves for the betterment of the community. Their kindness is appreciated by many, myself included.

Equally as important, thank you to Paul Berton, Editor-In-Chief at the London Free Press, for believing in me. He took a chance hiring me as a columnist before I had professional writing experience. I'll be forever grateful for his out-of-the-box thinking. As well, thank you to the rest of the team at the newspaper and at other media outlets who made writing four columns a week such an incredible adventure for me.

Most of all, thank you to those who are reading this publication. It's one thing to write a book; it's another to actually have people who want to read it! I sincerely hope its information will help you achieve success and build your own ultimate network.

Preface

Eight years ago my life was dramatically different.

Finding success in media, business and politics was merely a pipe dream whereas today, it's a reality. None of this would have been possible without the incredible people who influenced my life and became part of my ultimate network.

I floundered through my early twenties after moving to the city six years earlier for post secondary school. A long string of jobs including selling cars, retailing make-up and working in the hospitality industry led me to a position at a laser eye surgery clinic.

My life was fine. But "fine" was a long way from where I envisioned my life would, and should, be. Even at age 25 I felt I was in a rut. My life lacked purpose and direction and I wanted more.

Raising me in a small community, my parents set an example of how to live a rewarding, community-minded lifestyle. My father was a business professional and politician and my mother was a teacher involved in church and charitable activities. I fully intended to achieve similar success and felt I had the substance to do just that, but I had no idea where to start.

One day I took a leap of faith and applied for a job as the executive assistant to the vice-president of a building supply company. Not exactly an obvious place to find fulfillment, but my potential new boss was very charitably inclined and happened to be the incoming president of the local Chamber of Commerce.

I scheduled the afternoon off work at the eye clinic, put on my best (well, okay, my only) navy suit and went to the interview. An hour later I was offered the job.

In the coming months, my life shifted.

I watched my boss give back to the community, take many phone calls, go to umpteen events and reap the rewards of having a strong network. I quickly realized that *I* wanted to be the one with the network doing great work in the community – not the assistant to the one who was. Then, with another leap of faith, I left the company to find my own way.

So there I was, filled with big aspirations for a purposeful life, but unemployed – and unconnected.

On my father's advice, I reluctantly called an acquaintance in my city who had a cottage close to my childhood home. She graciously invited me to a political "meet and greet" she and her husband were hosting at his law firm that weekend. I didn't know what to expect so my parents agreed to come to the event to give me moral support.

I'll never forget that reception.

I collected several business cards and promised to connect with each contact the next week. While I was busy hunting for employment opportunities, my parents were volunteering me for political and charitable projects. By the end of that reception, "I" had agreed to get involved in a political campaign and join some mysterious gala committee.

To start my gala work, I had to return to the law office the next Tuesday to meet the senior law partner so we could drive to the meeting together. Talk about venturing into unknown territory. I spent the whole morning getting ready...ultimately choosing to wear the same navy suit I had worn less than a year earlier for my interview.

On the ride to the meeting, it was all I could do to keep from sweating through my suit while remembering to breathe as I listened to the classical music on his car radio. The whole time I questioned in my mind why this accomplished lawyer would invite me to work on this committee. I assumed he was posing the same question in his mind as I, the apparent mute, rode beside him. I felt completely out of my comfort zone.

I don't even know why I was so nervous. It didn't make sense. Looking back, I think it was because it was my first time officially flying solo. I didn't have an "assistant" title to hide behind or my parents' coat tails to ride – it was just me. I was 25 and it was show time.

The committee members were incredibly friendly and welcoming. As we started to discuss the fundraiser, I found myself saying, "Oh I know him; I'd be happy to make the call".

That's when I realized I had already started to build my network at my previous job. Since I'd left on good terms and had projected a professional image as an assistant, when I did call, the contacts were more than happy to help me collect auction items for the charity gala.

The contacts I met at the political reception and my first committee meeting are still some of my best friends, business associates and political supporters. Those few hours changed my life's path and led me to where I am today.

It didn't take long for the power of networking to become crystal clear to me. I was experiencing how one person could lead to another person who leads to the next person who positively influences your life.

Shortly after, thanks to my connections, I landed a job in the not-for-profit sector, became involved with several organizations and earned a spot on a political party's Provincial executive. Within 18 months my Rolodex (electronic filing systems weren't widely used then) went from having a few cards to being overloaded with hundreds of new contacts. Within another few years that number grew to several thousand contacts.

During a phone call to a member of my newly established network, I learned about a columnist position becoming available at the city's daily newspaper. Within a few months my first column was published.

Four years later, I succumbed to my passion for politics and resigned from the newspaper to run as a political candidate in the Provincial election. My party didn't win the general election, but my involvement in the process was an incredible experience.

Writing for the newspaper, running for public office, holding high-profile positions, building a company and finding purpose and fulfillment in life would never have been possible if I hadn't learned how to build a strong professional network and expand my circles of influence.

Building a network with thousands of quality contacts in such a short period of time wasn't an easy task. I remember one year that was especially hectic. In addition to running a company, writing my four weekly columns, working in radio and television, and volunteering for several organizations, I attended just shy of 250 events. Add the effort needed to manage the network of contacts while finding time for a personal life, and you can imagine that my schedule was fairly intense.

Working at that intensity level is not required to build the ultimate network. In fact, I don't recommend that pace for anyone (myself included). But those interactions, combined with my varied professional and personal experiences, have given me the foundation for my consulting and speaking work and for writing this book.

Introduction

As a professional you likely attend, or plan to attend, business functions in an effort to expand your network. But why?

Are you truly connecting with people or are you just putting in time?

We spend our adult lives interacting with people to earn our living, but shockingly, throughout years of schooling there is no course dedicated to teaching us these specific skills to help us connect with others and build our networks.

As humans we naturally engage in networking on some level, but when the word is formalized as a business activity, for some, it conjures a vision of calculation and manipulation.

Proper networking, the kind that's taught in this book, elicits the exact opposite response. It's not a cheesy sales technique, but rather a genuine attempt to connect with others and to let others connect with you.

Sales trainers will inevitably tell you to build your network to generate business leads. Job hunting manuals will tell you to tap into your network to get your application to the top of the resumé pile. Company leaders will tell their junior associates to get "out there" and build their network.

It all sounds great in theory, but the question is, "How?" Where do you go to build your network and once you're there, what do you do so that you're not just collecting business cards? What is the secret to turning those casual business card contacts into long-term, mutually beneficial relationships?

There was a time when I struggled to answer these same questions.

After achieving success in business, politics and the media as a direct result of developing a strong professional network, all the while hearing the woes of others who struggle with the concept, I recognized the need to define a step-by-step process to help other professionals get connected.

Before I launched my training and consulting company, people would ask me for advice on how to get connected and I was happy to oblige. For some, a little advice was all the help needed and they were off to build their network and achieve success.

Others weren't so agreeable – or successful. After showing up once or twice to events, they'd tell me networking doesn't work. They would lose sight of their reasons for wanting a strong network and quit.

This result puzzled me. Of course networking works – I was living proof. I knew that networking, when done properly and professionally, is an amazingly powerful tool that will enable a person to achieve whatever can be imagined.

So why then, do so many professionals struggle to make networking work for them while others find success with it?

It became my professional mission to find tangible answers to this question so that I could give solutions to help others fast track their success by learning how to connect with the world's greatest resource – people.

As I studied people whom I perceived to be master networkers, it was clear that most didn't consciously realize what they did to network. They found success by trial and error and by mirroring the behaviour of their mentors. For them, networking just came naturally.

Similarly, those who struggle with networking seem completely unaware of what they do to shoot themselves in the foot. Fortunately, some self-awareness and technique-tweaking are all it takes to re-aim the gun barrel from down at the foot to the bull's eye.

This book is overflowing with information that will help you build your ultimate network. The ideas presented are a culmination of extensive research into best practices for networking. Most importantly, they are lessons learned from my personal experience interacting and connecting with thousands of people over the last several years.

Whether you are just beginning your career or whether you already have a strong foundation on which to build, these concepts, when applied, are proven to help professionals get connected and achieve success.

Those new to networking may find the information overwhelming, so read the book, do the exercises and then revisit the concepts as you grow your network. Over time these strategies will make sense.

Those with substantial networking experience are invited to read the book with an open mind. Consider your own personal journey and how these concepts apply to you. Stick with what's working and fine-tune areas that need improvement to maximize your efforts.

As you read this book, you'll realize I am far from perfect. There are days when my foot finds a comfortable resting place in my mouth and I add another experience to my tally of embarrassing moments – some of which I share throughout this book. Being prepared for the unexpected, accepting yourself for who you are at each moment, having a keen sense of humour and offering forgiveness for yourself and others can go a long way to help you enjoy the process of building your professional network.

I wish you all the best as you work to achieve your ultimate network. It will take time and effort, but it will be well worth the investment. I love to hear stories so please visit my website, www.elevatebiz.ca, to share your tales of success – and your blunders too.

Section 1
The Concept

1 Building the Ultimate Network

H ave you ever noticed the most successful people also seem to be the most connected? After interacting and connecting with thousands of people, I have yet to meet a truly talented networker who is unsuccessful.

Think about it: nothing happens without people making it happen. The more people a person is positively connected to, the more opportunities he will have. The law of averages means that getting connected will put you in an advantageous position both personally and professionally.

Looking back, every exciting and challenging twist in my career was instigated by a connection with another professional. Most likely, when you look back on your life you will find the same to be true.

In their book, *Middle-Class Millionaire*, authors Russ Alan Prince and Lewis Schiff[1] studied the behaviours and characteristics that separate the regular middle class from those who elevated themselves to achieve millionaire status. Their research identified four key elements that define the Middle-Class Millionaire: hard work, financial savvy, persistence and *networking*.

In addition to being a fascinating read, for me this book solidified the importance of networking and its impact on the average person's ability to achieve optimal success. If your goal is to become a millionaire, then according to their in-depth research, mastering the art of business networking is one of four proficiencies that can make that dream a reality.

Whatever you want to accomplish can be done provided you surround yourself with the right people. Surely you've heard the saying, "It's not what you know, it's who you know and who knows you". Building the ultimate network means more people will know you and you will know more people.

"

Whatever you want to accomplish can be done provided you surround yourself with the right people.

"

This book is not about collecting business cards and simply adding names to your database. You could have 10,000 names in your address book, but if you're not connected with those people and they don't know who you are, what's the point?

When done properly and professionally, networking will help you turn those casual business card contacts into long-term, mutually beneficial business relationships.

This book is divided into four key sections: The Concept, The Business of YOU, The Fundamentals and The Strategy. Each section builds on the next so by the end of the book you will have all the tools necessary to develop your ultimate network.

SECTION 1: THE CONCEPT

This section will help shape your perspective on business networking by defining what it is and what it is not. It will solidify your overall goals and objectives, outline realistic expectations and identify common mistakes that can keep you from truly connecting with others.

SECTION 2: THE BUSINESS OF YOU

This is where we'll address and develop your personal brand to ensure you are attracting new business relationships by conveying a genuine, welcoming, professional image that is essential to your success.

SECTION 3: THE FUNDAMENTALS

These are the everyday elements that we're just expected to know, but are rarely taught. Mastering the fundamentals will give you confidence and add an extra notch of professionalism to your image. When used correctly and effectively, these basics can be your most valuable assets as you build your ultimate network.

SECTION 4: THE STRATEGY

Once you are ready to share the Business of YOU and you've mastered the Fundamentals, this section is where you'll learn to develop a strategy to make your ultimate network a reality.

Building your ultimate network is not rocket science. It's simply connecting with people and letting people connect with you. This book will give you the tools to do exactly that. Once you've figured out how to connect with the world's greatest resource, people, then you can start to see the world's population as one big game of connect the dots.

The possibilities are infinite!

2 What Does the Ultimate Network Mean to You?

> **"**
>
> **The benefits of networking have a domino effect. You can't experience one advantage without others falling into place.**
>
> **"**

Envision the possibilities if you add hundreds of quality contacts to your personal network. Would your life be different? Would achieving success be easier and happen faster? The answer to these questions is, "Yes".

Since you're reading this book, it's clear you have a desire to build your network and expand your circles of influence. There is a myriad of reasons why you've made this decision. It would be impossible for me to guess your specific motivation, but I suspect it falls into one of three categories – you're looking to enhance your professional results, improve your quality of life – or both.

Although you may have a specific goal in mind, the benefits of networking have a domino effect. You can't experience one advantage without others falling into place.

Here are just some tangible and intangible benefits you can look forward to when you expand your network:

- having a sense of purpose
- living a happier life
- always knowing who to call when you have a need
- being in a position to help people by connecting them with others
- being seen as a leader in your community and/or industry
- making it easy to break into a new city or group of people
- experiencing company growth
- creating new friendships
- elevating your confidence
- eliminating the hit-and-miss application and interview process
- getting your charity to the top of the donor request pile
- earning goodwill with your contacts
- amplifying public awareness
- seeing increased referrals
- knowing everyone in a room and everyone knowing you
- generating new clients
- growing personally
- developing a positive reputation
- gaining professional development
- advertising through word of mouth
- creating company buzz
- finding mentors
- becoming a mentor for others

The ultimate network means different things to different people. The most important question is, "What does it mean to you?".

Close your eyes and imagine your life once you've built the ultimate network. What are you hoping to achieve? Who do you want to know? What do you wish to accomplish that you can't now without the ultimate network?

_____

_____

_____

_____

_____

Take a mental snapshot of your life with the ultimate network. Write down your vision and keep your answer front and centre in your life. Place your post-it note on your bathroom mirror or beside your computer screen.

Identifying your vision and what you ultimately want to achieve will give you a point of reference that will motivate you as you build your network.

Years ago a friend said to me, "When my head hits the pillow at night, I want to be sure it deserves the rest." I thought this line captured the meaning of a purposeful life, so when I decided to take my life in a more fulfilling direction I wrote, "Deserve to hit the pillow" on my post-it note.

Now I have a post-it note in my office that says, "Make Your Mark" because it sums up what I want to do – make my mark on the world and help others do the same.

Your vision statement doesn't have to be profound, just something that reminds you of your long-term vision to give you an extra boost of energy.

MY VISION STATEMENT

_____

_____

_____

_____

3 What Networking is Not

The best way to truly understand business networking is to first understand what it is not.

Misconceptions and negative connotations associated with networking are caused by bad experiences with unprofessional networkers who confuse "networking" with "selling". These are two distinct activities. However, far too often over-eager professionals blur the line between building relationships and entering the sales process.

When done properly and professionally, networking will eventually lead to new sales contracts, make sales easier and make referrals more abundant, but those benefits are merely by-products of an ultimate network. There is so much more to it.

Understanding the concept that selling and networking are two different activities was the turning point for a client who is the vice-president of an investment firm. Before he came to this realization, it was like pulling teeth to get him to engage in networking, even though his role required his presence in the community.

He was under the impression that each time he went out to an event, he had to catch a new client hook, line and sinker. No wonder he wasn't comfortable with networking – that's a lot of pressure. Changing his perspective allowed him to genuinely enjoy the process of connecting with others.

Going to networking events expecting to land new clients or sell your product is setting yourself up for failure and frustration. This misguided philosophy permeates networking events every day.

> **Going to networking events expecting to land new clients or sell your product is setting yourself up for failure and frustration.**

Shortly after an introduction, if a person rushes into a sales pitch without qualification of interest, need or fit for the product or service being sold, then the opportunity to build a relationship is missed because no one likes to be "sold" or feel "cornered".

This doesn't mean you should never enter the sales process after meeting a new contact. If a person self-identifies as a potential client or there is an obvious fit to collaborate on a venture, then yes, the sales process and/or an appropriate course of action should begin. (Refer to Chapter 53, Categorizing Contacts).

When this obvious link does not exist it's more important to focus on the development of a long-term relationship rather than making the sale. Over time, as you learn more about each other and establish a deeper bond, opportunities to work together will likely present themselves naturally.

An associate dropped out of the "mainstream circuit" for a couple of years while he changed jobs and solidified his path. We ran into each other at a reception and I was sincerely pleased to hear he'd found passion and purpose through his new venture. He asked me to go for coffee so we could visit about life since we'd last seen each other.

The "visit" started off well. It was a normal "get-reconnected" meeting in my mind. Suddenly the tone changed. I quickly understood our get-reconnected meeting was actually a "sales" meeting – two totally different things.

For 45 minutes he went into an elaborate sales pitch. He not only wanted me to become his client; he also wanted me to refer him to others.

Finally he came up for air and I was able to explain that I wasn't a qualified client. This was crucial information he would have known had he spent time asking me questions and listening to my answers or been up front about his true intentions when we booked the meeting.

Time is valuable so to spend time listening to a pitch that had no relevance to me was simply annoying. I felt duped.

If this had been my first exposure to the "networking process", I would have been completely turned off because he hid behind the guise of networking when truthfully he was in full sales mode.

On another occasion, a gentleman asked me to meet with him to discuss his business and to see if I could help. The expectation in this situation was clear from the onset so there were no uncomfortable sales-pitch surprises. Even though there wasn't a fit for me with his company, I was able and pleased to connect him with others who were better matched for his needs.

Two different meetings with different tactics, therefore, different results. Be up front and clear about your intentions for meeting rather than using backdoor smoke and mirror tactics.

> **"**
>
> **Be up front and clear about your intentions for meeting rather than using backdoor smoke and mirror tactics.**
>
> **""**

Agenda-pushing also contributes to networking's bad name. In life everyone has his own agenda. The sooner you understand that your agenda is not the same as anyone else's, the easier it will be for you to take a step back and genuinely connect with people.

Another person's priorities are rarely exactly in line with yours. Hitting a year-end sales target or raising money for a charity would rank differently for you, the seller or fundraiser, than for the potential buyer or donor. Accepting this natural variance in priorities will help you identify the appropriate pace for building a relationship. Pushing your agenda onto someone else is a surefire way to ignite the "fight or flight" response in others.

When inevitable year-end crunch times occur, that's when you tap into your existing network, not when you try to push new contacts into your master plan.

There is a distinction between trying to close a deal with a new contact at a networking function versus calling an established associate and asking to be referred to someone who may need your product or service.

Another negative networking image comes from those who try too hard. The overt social climbers anxious to arrive at a new station in life are easily spotted. People can smell a phoney a mile away. Phoniness is not an attribute that encourages meaningful connections.

If, before reading this book, you have developed a negative impression of networking, either because you have been on the receiving end of unprofessional networking tactics or because you have been guilty of blurring these lines yourself, the time has come to accept and erase any such connotations.

A negative impression doesn't diminish the importance of networking and the positive impact proper networking can have on your life. You can't change the past. The key is to focus on the future. Even if you feel like you've "blown it", don't worry; you can recover!

Understanding common behavioural culprits that hinder networking success will help you avoid making these mistakes in the future and will set you on a path to become a master networker.

4 Understanding Business Networking

To solidify in your mind the essence of business networking, consider the famous quote by author and businessman Mark McCormack: "All things being equal, people will do business with a friend. All things being unequal, people will still do business with a friend."

I doubt he was suggesting that you have to be best friends with everyone you hope will buy your product or service. That's not realistic, but there has to be something that distinguishes you from your competition. That something is a relationship or what I like to refer to as a "mini-bond". You're not best friends (at least not yet), but you have connected and established a sense of comfort that creates an environment for a positive business association to be pursued.

For those who network well, creating this environment is a natural part of doing business – it just happens. With some *perspective*, *preparation* and *practice*, you too will achieve this sense of ease with your business networking efforts.

By definition, networking is the gathering of acquaintances or contacts – the building up or maintaining of informal relationships, especially with people whose friendship could bring advantages such as job or business opportunities.[2]

Bottom line, networking is all about connecting with others and letting others connect with you. From there, anything can happen.

As we determined in the previous chapter, networking is not selling, nor is it a chance to push your own agenda. With that in mind, you may wonder how networking can generate business growth.

To sell your product or service, you first need customers who are willing to buy. Once they know your product exists, they must decide to buy from you instead of your competition. There are only a handful of ways to engage people in this decision-making process.

> **"**
>
> **Networking is all about connecting with others and letting others connect with you.**
>
> **"**

One way to generate new business leads is through advertising. Not everyone has huge budgets to run massive ad campaigns that will entice potential customers to choose you over your competition. It's the most costly option and if the other guy launches a bigger and better advertising campaign, you're likely out of luck.

Two other options to generate new client leads are direct marketing and cold calling. Not everyone is comfortable using these tactics, nor does everyone have the patience and staying power to work the numbers that these techniques require. You can expect less than one per cent return from your efforts and expenses using these strategies.

The above options have you appealing to the masses and hoping to catch potential clients at the perfect time so they proactively seek to do business with you. There are certain industries that lend themselves well to such macro campaigns.

Large companies, such as banks, are a great example. They can run huge advertising campaigns, but still, when it comes to earning the business at the grassroots level, relationships become more important. If you know, like and trust the bank manager at one branch, you are more likely to choose to do business there, rather than across the street with his competition.

In the end, networking is the most effective way to generate new business leads. Networking, done properly and professionally, will lead to new contacts who want to do business with you. It creates word of mouth buzz, attracts referrals and generates loyalty. As a person responsible for generating new business development, what more could you ask?

There are two overall objectives for business networking:

1   When you have a need, you know who to call and when you do, he or she will want to pick up the phone to talk with you.

2   When your contacts need your product or service, they will think to call or recommend you first.

Imagine how much easier life would be if, whenever you were looking for a solution, you only had to look to your personal address book to find the answer. With a strong professional network, you're only a couple of calls away from whomever you need to meet. Your relationship may not seal the deal, but it should at least get you in the door.

Imagine if your contacts immediately thought of you whenever a personal or professional situation arose. It doesn't matter what you do, the principle remains the same. If you're an insurance advisor, financial broker, accountant, lawyer, car salesman, hairdresser, dance teacher, graphic designer or any other professional with competition, you want to be sure that your contacts will think of you first as the potential solution provider for their needs.

That's the power of networking!

> **"**
>
> **Networking, done properly and professionally, will lead to new contacts who want to do business with you. It creates word of mouth buzz, attracts referrals and generates loyalty.**
>
> **"**

5 Education and Connection

Networking is an exercise in education and connection.

It is your responsibility to educate your contacts about who you are, what you do and what you have to offer. It is also your responsibility to connect with others so they want to do business with you.

If your contacts call your competition instead of you, chances are you're missing the education and connection components. That's not their fault. You are the one at fault because you didn't give them the information and/or the comfort level they needed to choose to work with you.

It's unrealistic to think that people will randomly pick up the phone to hire you if they haven't met you personally or heard of you through one of their trusted contacts. Nor can they be expected to call you if they don't understand what product or service you offer and recognize your value.

There are people who will circulate the networking scene for years, but don't clearly communicate who they are or what they do. They keep their "cards" close to their chest, possibly in an effort to avoid appearing pushy or too eager for a sale.

This subdued approach leaves money on the table because even though people may like you, they won't know and understand enough about what you do and what you have to offer to decide to do business with you.

We will discuss specifics on how to communicate the Business of YOU in Section 3, but for now, just understand: it is your responsibility to make it easy for people to know who you are, what you do and what you have to offer.

As you build your ultimate network, it's equally important for you to grasp who is in your professional network. Who do you know, what do they do and what do they have to offer? Knowing who is accessible to you will make it easier for you to find solutions and connect others.

> **To build your ultimate network, you'll need to project a genuine, welcoming, professional image that will encourage people to like you, trust you and think you are competent.**

Once people know you, it's essential that they like you, trust you and think you are competent. Otherwise, why would they do business with you?

If you walk around like a pompous diva, it's unlikely folks will want to connect with you. If you tend to exaggerate and over-promise at meetings then fail to deliver, it'll be tough for them to think you are trustworthy. If you're the drunken guy who flipped the golf cart at the last charity tournament, envisioning you as a competent businessman becomes a bit of a stretch.

To build your ultimate network, you'll need to project a genuine, welcoming, professional image that will encourage people to like you, trust you and think you are competent.

It can be difficult to take a look in the mirror and honestly dissect the image we portray. Habits formed over a lifetime can unknowingly block our ability to connect with others. Identifying and changing these behaviours, as will be discussed in Section 2, can be difficult, but are imperative steps if you wish to connect with others to establish your ultimate network.

6 Expectations

My clients come to me because they have struggled, often for years, to create a solid network that leads to personal and professional fulfillment. They are fully aware that they need to network and know it works for others, but haven't made it work for themselves – yet.

My job is to help them find the reason they're missing the mark and help them tweak their behaviours accordingly.

Behaviours that hinder networking success are fairly universal. It's usually one or a combination of two or more of these four culprits:

- not having realistic expectations (Section 1: The Concept)
- not portraying a genuine, welcoming, professional image that invites new relationships and encourages people to like you, trust you and think you are competent (Section 2: The Business of YOU)
- not making it easy for people to know who you are, what you do and what you have to offer (Section 3: The Fundamentals)
- not having enough meaningful interaction with enough of the right people (Section 4: The Strategy)

To change results we must first adjust our expectations. People who show up once or twice and get frustrated because they haven't seen any tangible results from their networking efforts are setting themselves up for failure.

Networking is not a quick fix. Getting to know people and letting them get to know you will require time. That's not to say that amazing things can't happen very quickly once you begin to interact with new contacts. They absolutely can. You never know whom you may meet.

However, it's best to have realistic expectations and practise patience as you build your ultimate network and expand your circles of influence. In time, you will achieve your vision.

Accept that you won't know everyone in a room the first time you walk into a function, but over time, with consistent and persistent effort, you will get to know more and more people and eventually feel like you belong. Expect that a room full of strangers will remain a room full of strangers until you meet and connect with them.

> **It is wise to adopt a slow and steady pace that will earn you a positive reputation and allow the natural development of solid relationships.**

It is wise to adopt a slow and steady pace that will earn you a positive reputation and allow the natural development of solid relationships.

After six months of business networking done properly and professionally, you'll create some momentum, make some initial contacts and develop a sense of comfort and belonging.

After 12 to 18 months of consistent and persistent effort you will notice a significant difference in your professional network. That's when the magic really starts to happen.

In five years you will notice your life has taken an entire shift for the better and you should be well on your way to embracing your ultimate network.

About a year and a half ago I met with a contact for coffee. He was the sole advisor for a finance company's satellite office. He was quite frustrated with his slow start, so we discussed the importance of patience and revisited his vision for the long haul. He reluctantly accepted the reality that building his business network would take longer than he wanted.

> **It takes six to eight casual encounters with someone before you hit his radar screen and he starts to "get" who you are.**

Approximately six months ago I saw him at an event and he pulled me aside to tell me that after a year of consistent and persistent effort, suddenly business was falling into place. Just recently I saw him again and he said his business was booming. Finally, he felt his efforts were rewarded. Had he given up when he first had doubts, he wouldn't be reaping the benefits now.

A year or two may seem like a long time to wait, but do you plan to still be in business in 12 to 18 months? Your current investment will lay the foundation for future business relationships. The work required to build a sustainable network is nothing compared to struggling through your professional life "unconnected."

It takes six to eight casual encounters with someone before you hit his radar screen and he starts to "get" who you are. It takes even longer for you to generate a sense of trust and competency that will lead to significant relationships. Connecting on a deeper level than just saying, "Hi" at a business reception can lessen this number, but even then it still takes multiple interactions with a new contact before you can expect to truly connect.

Think about how many people you've met, had lunch with or even sat next to in a boardroom and yet have forgotten. Yes, this is a trick question because I'm asking you to remember something you've forgotten, but it makes the point.

Not everyone we meet in passing makes a lasting impression on us and vice-versa. Expecting contacts to remember you after one or two introductions can add frustration to networking and chip away at your self-confidence. It's not necessarily a reflection of how memorable you are, but rather the reality of society's hectic pace.

You may find that it takes longer to develop relationships with more established leaders and accomplished networkers. They tend to have a healthy level of skepticism about newbie-networkers who flash onto the scene in a "here today, gone tomorrow" fashion. Over the years we've seen many who, after a whirlwind presence, drop off the face of the earth until they randomly resurface a year or two later.

This kind of inconsistency detracts from a person's trust factor and diminishes his ability to connect with those who have a more consistent track record.

For better or worse, a person's true colours start to show after five or six months, so instinctively, people tend to keep guarded from new contacts for at least that amount of time. It's easy for someone to put on an act for six months, which is why the six-month mark in any relationship is so critical. After that time, familiarity sets in, barriers break down and true personalities either shine – or tarnish.

> **"**
>
> **You can't force the natural pace of any one relationship, so to build your network faster you will have to increase the number of people with whom you connect.**
>
> **"**

If you're like I am and patience is not your greatest virtue, then you'll be pleased to know there is a way to speed up the networking process. You need to do more of it. You can't force the natural pace of any one relationship, so to build your network faster you will have to increase the number of people with whom you connect. Some relationships will happen quickly; others will take longer to grow. It can be done because as you've read, I reaped the benefits of networking in a very short period of time. But I jumped in with both feet, met a ridiculous number of people and worked intensely to make it happen. This book will give you the tools to do the same, but be careful; you still need the mind-set that you're in this for the long haul or you'll lack credibility.

Achieving your ultimate network could take years. How many? Who knows? I can't say. It depends on your definition of the ultimate network and the many factors that affect your ability to connect with others. No matter how long it requires, take it from someone who has benefited extensively from the power of networking: it will be well worth your investment of time, energy and money. Stick with it. Your efforts in the short term will pay dividends in the future.

↗ Section 1 Summary

- Anything you want to achieve can be accomplished by surrounding yourself with the right people and learning how to connect with the world's greatest resource – people!

- You can become a master networker with some proper perspective, preparation and practice.

- Business networking is all about connecting with others and letting others connect with you.

- There are two overall objectives for business networking: 1. When you have a need, you know who to call and when you do, he will want to pick up the phone to talk with you. 2. When your contacts need your product or service, they will think to call or recommend you first.

- Networking is not selling. It is an exercise in education and connection.

- It is your responsibility to make it easy for people to know who you are, what you do and what you have to offer.

- It is imperative that you project a genuine, welcoming, professional image that will encourage people to like you, trust you and think you are competent.

- Understand the classic mistakes that hinder business networking success so you can avoid them and maximize your results.

- Be up front and clear about your intentions when meeting with contacts.

- You can't force the natural pace of any one relationship. To build your network faster you will have to increase the number of people with whom you connect.

- It takes six to eight times of meeting someone casually before you "get" who he is and vice-versa.

- You will experience networking momentum after six months of consistent and persistent effort. In 12 to 18 months you will be well on your way to reaping the rewards from your ultimate network.

Section 2
The Business of YOU

7 The Business of YOU

A s you build your ultimate network and expand your circles of influence, the image you project will either help or hinder your business networking efforts. By addressing your personal brand, or what I like to call the Business of YOU, up front, you will increase your ability to connect with others. Taking steps to optimize the Business of YOU will enhance your business networking efforts as well as make a positive impact on other aspects of your life.

No doubt you've heard the term "branding." You can't take a marketing class without touching on the concept and companies spend thousands and in some cases millions of dollars to develop corporate brands.

Marty Neumeier, author of "The Zag and the Brand Gap", summed up the brand concept best: "A brand is a person's gut feeling about a product, service or company. It's not what you say it is – it's what they say it is. The best you can do is influence it."[3]

The irony is that companies spend all that money developing a corporate brand, but ultimately it's the people who represent the company who make the most significant contribution to influencing a company's brand. If a person answers the company phone rudely, the negative experience will naturally influence a customer's gut feeling, regardless of what the latest advertisement says. Individual reputations have a ripple effect on a company's brand. Therefore, a corporate brand is really the sum of all the personal brands that represent it.

National and international companies are at the mercy of their local representatives. It's the people at the ground level who are the face of the organization and who ultimately connect with current and potential clients – a scary thought if you're the president of a major company with thousands of employees.

> **Individual reputations have a ripple effect on a company's brand. Therefore, a corporate brand is really the sum of all the personal brands that represent it.**

Thankfully, for most of us our livelihood is not in the hands of thousands, but it is in our own two hands. It's important to comprehend the enormous impact a personal brand has on your ability to connect and succeed.

The smaller the organization, the more a person's reputation contributes to the public's perception or gut feeling about the company. If you're the president of your own business, your company's brand is directly impacted by others' gut reactions about you.

Don't underestimate the power the Business of YOU has on making or breaking your future. Each and every time you interact with others, they are forming an opinion about you consciously or subconsciously that will add to, reinforce or subtract from whether they like you, trust you and think you are competent.

These opinions are formed based on intangible perceptions that generate another's gut feeling about you – which equates to your personal brand – which equates to your company brand.

The key to developing your personal brand and optimizing the Business of YOU starts with self-awareness. What you have done in the past, what you are doing today and what you will do tomorrow all affect how you are perceived by others.

Years ago, when I sold cars, my boss would say, "A customer's perception is his reality." How true. When you think about the impression you make, it's really not about what you think the impression is. The impression you make is what others think it is.

> **"**
>
> **Each and every time you interact with others, they are forming an opinion about you consciously or subconsciously that will add to, reinforce or subtract from whether they like you, trust you and think you are competent.**
>
> **"**

As we move through the coming chapters to develop the Business of YOU your job is two-fold:

1. Identify your strengths so you can maximize what's working.

2. Identify areas that need improvement so you can make adjustments to put yourself in a position to win.

The objective is not to change your personality. You are who you are and that's exactly who you need to be to build your ultimate network. The goal is to tweak any behaviours that may keep you from connecting with others and growing your ultimate network.

Major red flags with your attitude or behaviour need to be identified and corrected right away. For the most part, making hasty changes in your life can be overwhelming and ineffective for the long term. It could cause you to focus too much on who you want to become rather than who you are.

Gradual changes work best. Incorporate one or two ideas every couple of weeks until you have achieved your desired image. Adjustments to optimize the Business of YOU are a balancing act, but over time, they will all fall into place.

8 Overcoming Age Objections

An investment advisor in her mid-30s asked me how, as a young professional, she can connect with older, more established potential clients with money. She joked that you need grey hair to be taken seriously in the financial world. That's not the case at all.

Many young professionals I speak with offer a similar sentiment, regardless of their line of work. It's easy to use age as an excuse to avoid building the ultimate network, but you'll miss amazing opportunities. There is a wealth of wisdom to gain from the elders who are anxious to impart their knowledge on up-and-comers.

Having youth on your side can be a huge asset as you build your professional network. Starting early means you have years to develop and solidify relationships plus, those who have been around longer appreciate a fresh face. On the flip side, someone who is more established, has more personal experiences from which to draw. It's never too late to build your ultimate network.

Your age, young or old, should not be a deterrent provided you back your image with substance.

At age 25, I was the youngest person in the room for my first gala committee meeting. Arguably, I was completely out of my element. My saving grace was that at the next meeting I returned with a completed to-do list. That earned me credibility and once you have that, age is no longer a factor.

At 32 years old I ran for a seat in the provincial legislature. I finally succumbed to my passion for politics, but first I had to win the nomination from the former MPP who was hoping to run again. It was a true clash between older versus younger, established versus new.

I always knew I would run for public office, but truth be told, I always figured it would be later in my life. Circumstances determined that it wasn't and ultimately it worked out in my favour.

When I announced my intentions to run, a politically astute man said, "The only challenge I see with your candidacy is your age and the only thing that will cure that is time." Arguably, I've packed more into my limited years than some people will in 90. As individuals, we have no control over our age. We only have control over what we do with the years we've lived.

> **"**
>
> **As individuals, we have no control over our age. We only have control over what we do with the years we've lived.**
>
> **"**

Thanks to my substantial network I was surrounded by amazing supporters who were as committed to winning the nomination as I was, but still, we were up against a worthy opponent with decades of loyalty in the riding and two terms of actual parliamentary experience.

In the end it was my nomination speech that tipped the ballots and led to my victory. Those who didn't know me saw that I was a credible candidate when I nailed my speech. As I calmly and confidently addressed the hundreds of people in the room, they stopped worrying about my age and focused on my message.

We didn't win the general election but it wasn't for lack of effort or enthusiasm. The months leading up to the election were spent connecting with voters and I earned a reputation as a hardworking, genuine candidate. When my age was mentioned, as it often was, my response was simply, "I'm not nearly as young as I look." That usually got a chuckle and then we would discuss pressing issues relevant to the political landscape of the day.

Hundreds of people of all ages helped with my campaign in varying capacities. One of the campaign's most dependable volunteers was 15 years old. His father was active politically and saw the value of his son getting experience in the political realm. Some were surprised to see such a young volunteer in the group, but as far as I was concerned, he was someone I could count on to always arrive on time, as promised, and with a smile on his face. When he interacted with people, he was polite, articulate and truly knowledgeable of the party's platform. His admirable qualities are rare in people at any age. You see, it's not the age of a person that matters — it's whether you like him, trust him and think he's competent.

> **"**
> **It's not the age of a person that matters — it's whether you like him, trust him and think he is competent.**
> **"**

Those are the necessary factors that influence and overcome concerns caused by obvious superficialities such as age.

Success does not magically begin once you cross a specific age threshold. It can happen at any age. Sure, longevity can give you experience, perspective, wisdom, credibility and a whole host of other benefits but there are many people much older than you who still haven't scratched the surface on building their professional networks.

> **"**
> **Success does not magically begin once you cross a specific age threshold. It can happen at any age.**
> **"**

You can be 55 years old, but if you're a crook you won't generate a feeling of trustworthiness. Equally, if you're 24 years old and you deliver on your promises and present a professional image, you will earn your place as a serious contender in life.

A professional network with a solid foundation will include people from all ages. It's a natural tendency to associate with people who are similar in age and station in life. These people will likely represent the bulk of your network, but don't be afraid to expand your comfort zone to include interactions with people outside of your natural sphere of influence. Expanding your horizons to connect with people from different ages and walks of life will be key to creating your ultimate network.

Those who are more senior will offer great insight and perspective concerning life and success. Thanks to a few more years, they will have more contacts and a stronger network, plus a lot more experience they can share.

At the very least find one person who is older and wiser to act as a mentor as you grow your career. Connections with this person can ignite your networking success and your overall personal and professional growth.

Some of my most treasured relationships are with people who are much older. Without their wisdom, counsel and support, my past, present and future journeys wouldn't be possible.

By the same token, younger contacts will infuse enthusiasm into your life. Being a mentor to an up-and-comer can give you fulfillment, and in the long run will open an entire new network of contacts for you.

How you interact with people at opposite ends of the age spectrum will adjust, depending on the nature of the relationship and the environment in which you are meeting. A formal black tie affair elicits a different response than a charity volleyball game with a bunch of buddies from school.

As a young professional, the image you project, regardless of your environment, is even more important to earn credibility than it is for someone who is older. Dressing respectfully, articulating your thoughts clearly and acting professionally will go a long way to connect you with the establishment. Playing with your tongue ring, sporting an overgrown goatee or wearing pants with a waistline that drops to your thighs will make it difficult for people to see you as an equal in professional circles. Although these styles may fit with your usual crowd, to connect with others you need to be as relatable as possible. To be taken seriously all the pieces must fit, so make a point to maximize the Business of YOU.

9 You Never Know Who's Watching

One morning I was driving into a coffee shop drive-thru. The tight laneway with multiple entrances made the morning rush hour particularly challenging. As I was about to take my place in line, a man cut in front of me. Luckily, I wasn't in a rush, the sun was shining and a favourite song was playing on the radio. I just smiled and waved him through.

Not long after, I was introduced to a gentleman at a formal event. He asked me if I drove a particular kind and colour of car. He was correct, but I was surprised he knew this information. He explained that he was the guy who almost crashed into me at the drive-thru. He apologized for not seeing me and then commented on my friendly nature and positive response to what could have prompted a nasty fit of road rage.

Can you imagine the difference if I had opted for a negative – yet more common – response that morning?

The point is, you never know who's watching from the sidelines. Each interaction with a contact, regardless of the environment, will add to, reinforce or subtract from his opinion of you.

> **You never know who's watching from the sidelines.**

You never know who is standing behind you in a coffee shop line or sitting beside you at a hockey game. It could very well be the person you meet in the boardroom on Monday morning. It's not that you have to constantly watch over your shoulder; you just want to be aware of the image you portray when you're in public and how your actions contribute to your personal brand.

You can test yourself by asking, "If my most important client saw me acting like this, would that be okay?"

If you're getting drunk and making a scene in public on Friday night and on Monday trying to get an investor for your company, it is only a matter of time before the two worlds collide and your credibility is questioned.

Variations of the same story happen over and over again and chip away at the reputations of professionals everyday. It doesn't mean you can't have fun; just keep it in check. The more people you meet and the larger your professional network, the more likely you are to run into people in casual situations. Your image isn't just generated in boardrooms and at networking functions; it's a culmination of *all* interactions between you and your contacts.

That doesn't mean you need to dress in a pinstriped suit seven days a week or put on full make-up before you go to the corner store. However, you do want to be presentable, act appropriately for the situation and be courteous to others, regardless of where you are.

It's absolutely acceptable if you run into a business associate at the grocery store when you have two kids running in the aisle, a crying baby in one arm, a diaper bag falling out of the other and a pile of groceries overflowing your cart – that's life, that's genuine. Treating the cashier like she's a second class citizen is a whole different story.

When I worked in the laser eye surgery clinic, I gave a lot of latitude to patients because undergoing eye surgery is stressful and people respond to stress differently. There was one patient, however, who was very difficult. There were some complications with his procedure, all of which could be fixed over time.

It got to the point where none of the staff wanted to deal with him. He was generally rude and overly demanding. We would all but flip a coin to see who would take his call and I was usually the one who did.

The next thing you knew, my career had blossomed. I'd long since left the eye clinic and landed a coveted columnist role for the city's daily newspaper. Now this patient and I ran in the same social circles. The tables had turned. No longer was I a "little receptionist." In his mind, I now had the power of the pen.

We never discussed how we really knew each other, but every time I would see him, flashbacks of his impolite, unreasonable behaviour would cross my mind. As much as he kept a smile on his face for the people he thought were important, I knew his true colours.

Adopting a principle to treat everyone equally and with respect at all times will ensure that you are never caught in this uncomfortable position.

I'm reminded of a similar experience that happened when I was a waitress fresh out of post-secondary school. This story had a completely different outcome. There were two gentlemen who came to lunch every Friday. They arrived at noon, sat in the far corner booth and ordered a pitcher of Rickard's Red with a pizza to share while they talked business. They were always pleasant, even on the days when the restaurant was packed and the service was slower than they hoped.

Years later, one of the two gentlemen was a key member of the steering committee for the first golf tournament I worked on in my executive assistant's role. We were happy to recall our Friday afternoon conversations and since he and his associate had always treated me with respect, even though I was "just" a waitress, my gut feeling had always been, and continues to be, positive about the two. Likewise, because I treated them with respect when I was a waitress, they seem happy that my career has progressed.

10 Your Ideal Personal Brand

Developing your ideal personal brand is a process. To start, decide what you want your personal brand to be. When others have a gut reaction about you, what do you want their gut to say?

Close your eyes and imagine the Business of YOU five years from now. What adjectives do you want people to use to describe you? Consider your mentors and those you deem to be the most successful in your field. Ask yourself, "Who has it together? Why does this person win my admiration? What qualities or behaviours do I appreciate and want to emulate?"

Review the list of descriptives below for suggestions. Remember, these words may not necessarily be used to describe you today, but represent the ideal image you strive to project in the future.

> *Rate the importance of each descriptive on a scale of one to six as it relates to your ideal personal brand, six being extremely important, one being not important.*

	6	5	4	3	2	1	Priorities # 1-10
• adaptable	❏	❏	❏	❏	❏	❏	_____
• approachable	❏	❏	❏	❏	❏	❏	_____
• assured	❏	❏	❏	❏	❏	❏	_____
• aware	❏	❏	❏	❏	❏	❏	_____
• calm	❏	❏	❏	❏	❏	❏	_____
• community-minded	❏	❏	❏	❏	❏	❏	_____
• compelling	❏	❏	❏	❏	❏	❏	_____
• competent	❏	❏	❏	❏	❏	❏	_____
• competitive	❏	❏	❏	❏	❏	❏	_____
• confident	❏	❏	❏	❏	❏	❏	_____
• connected	❏	❏	❏	❏	❏	❏	_____
• contributor	❏	❏	❏	❏	❏	❏	_____
• dedicated	❏	❏	❏	❏	❏	❏	_____
• determined	❏	❏	❏	❏	❏	❏	_____
• easy going	❏	❏	❏	❏	❏	❏	_____
• engaging	❏	❏	❏	❏	❏	❏	_____
• enjoyable	❏	❏	❏	❏	❏	❏	_____

	6	5	4	3	2	1	Priorities # 1-10
• even-tempered	❏	❏	❏	❏	❏	❏	____
• environmentally friendly	❏	❏	❏	❏	❏	❏	____
• family-oriented	❏	❏	❏	❏	❏	❏	____
• flexible	❏	❏	❏	❏	❏	❏	____
• forgiving	❏	❏	❏	❏	❏	❏	____
• genuine	❏	❏	❏	❏	❏	❏	____
• good listener	❏	❏	❏	❏	❏	❏	____
• happy	❏	❏	❏	❏	❏	❏	____
• hard-working	❏	❏	❏	❏	❏	❏	____
• honest	❏	❏	❏	❏	❏	❏	____
• independent	❏	❏	❏	❏	❏	❏	____
• industry leader	❏	❏	❏	❏	❏	❏	____
• intelligent	❏	❏	❏	❏	❏	❏	____
• interested	❏	❏	❏	❏	❏	❏	____
• interesting	❏	❏	❏	❏	❏	❏	____
• mature	❏	❏	❏	❏	❏	❏	____
• non-aggressive	❏	❏	❏	❏	❏	❏	____
• patient	❏	❏	❏	❏	❏	❏	____
• polite	❏	❏	❏	❏	❏	❏	____
• positive	❏	❏	❏	❏	❏	❏	____

	6	5	4	3	2	1	Priorities # 1-10
• professional	❑	❑	❑	❑	❑	❑	_____
• put-together	❑	❑	❑	❑	❑	❑	_____
• realistic	❑	❑	❑	❑	❑	❑	_____
• relaxed	❑	❑	❑	❑	❑	❑	_____
• respectable	❑	❑	❑	❑	❑	❑	_____
• respectful of others	❑	❑	❑	❑	❑	❑	_____
• respectful of property	❑	❑	❑	❑	❑	❑	_____
• sets others at ease	❑	❑	❑	❑	❑	❑	_____
• stable	❑	❑	❑	❑	❑	❑	_____
• sophisticated	❑	❑	❑	❑	❑	❑	_____
• team-player	❑	❑	❑	❑	❑	❑	_____
• trustworthy	❑	❑	❑	❑	❑	❑	_____
• values-driven	❑	❑	❑	❑	❑	❑	_____
• welcoming	❑	❑	❑	❑	❑	❑	_____
• well-rounded	❑	❑	❑	❑	❑	❑	_____

Which descriptives do you value most? Once you've reviewed the list, prioritize the top 10 descriptives that you want to present to others through your behaviour. Next, narrow your top ten to the top five descriptives you want contacts to use to describe you.

TOP 5 DESCRIPTIVES FOR MY IDEAL BRAND

1 _____

2 _____

3 _____

4 _____

5 _____

Set aside your personal ideals for a moment and consider which are the most important qualities needed for your profession. Which ones will set you apart from your competition? What are the determining factors that will encourage people to want to do business with you? Are these qualities different than the 5 you indicated above? Are your expectations of yourself on a personal level different than in your professional capacity?

If so, write the descriptives you feel are required to be successful in your profession below.

ADDITIONAL DESCRIPTIVES FOR MY PROFESSIONAL BRAND

_____

_____

_____

Now that you know what you are striving to achieve, you can move to the next chapter where we'll look at your current reality.

11 Reality Check

Now that you've solidified the image you want to portray, it's time to consider the reality of today. Forget about what you want to portray; think about what you are actually portraying.

What would it be like to meet you?

Clients cringe at this question because they are often afraid to honestly consider their answer. Don't be nervous; this is not a "beat-yourself-up" session. This is an exercise in self-awareness that will ultimately lead to self-improvement. Now is the time to identify any potential behavioural culprits so that you can work to improve them.

> **What would it be like to meet you?**

Close your eyes and imagine you were just introduced to yourself. What impression would you make? If you met yourself, would you want to do business with you? Would you like you? Trust you? Think you are competent? Do the answers to these questions depend on the environment you are in at the time? Does the impression you make change with your mood?

How do others respond to meeting you? Do they engage in conversation with you or seem to not even notice you're there? Are they drawn to you? Are you approachable? Do you put people at ease or make them feel on edge? Are you interested and interesting? Are you argumentative or judgemental? Do you look professional or do you look like you just rolled out of bed? Do people back away from you? If so, are you invading their personal space by talking too closely or do you have bad breath or body odour?

Now that you're becoming aware of the Business of YOU, it's likely you will notice different reactions in different situations.

> *Write an initial list of descriptives that you believe portray you. Be honest. Next time you're in public take notice of how others react to you.*

DESCRIPTIVES THAT DEPICT THE REALITY OF ME

_____   _____

_____   _____

_____   _____

_____   _____

_____   _____

_____   _____

Consider the descriptives below and whether they apply to you rarely, often or depending on the situation.

	Rarely	Often	Depending on the Situation
• agenda-driven	❏	❏	❏
• aggressive	❏	❏	❏
• argumentative	❏	❏	❏
• bitter	❏	❏	❏
• controlling	❏	❏	❏
• dishonest	❏	❏	❏
• disorganized	❏	❏	❏
• disrespectful	❏	❏	❏
• diva-like	❏	❏	❏
• dramatic	❏	❏	❏
• gossipy	❏	❏	❏
• hesitant	❏	❏	❏

	Rarely	Often	Depending on the Situation
• immature	❏	❏	❏
• impolite	❏	❏	❏
• impulsive	❏	❏	❏
• inappropriate	❏	❏	❏
• incompetent	❏	❏	❏
• insincere	❏	❏	❏
• interrogator	❏	❏	❏
• invasive	❏	❏	❏
• irresponsible	❏	❏	❏
• judgmental	❏	❏	❏
• lacking confidence	❏	❏	❏
• messy	❏	❏	❏
• moody	❏	❏	❏
• nonchalant	❏	❏	❏
• pushy	❏	❏	❏
• self-absorbed	❏	❏	❏
• selfish	❏	❏	❏
• shy	❏	❏	❏
• smelly	❏	❏	❏
• stand-offish	❏	❏	❏
• stressed	❏	❏	❏
• unapproachable	❏	❏	❏
• unaware	❏	❏	❏
• uncertain	❏	❏	❏
• unhappy	❏	❏	❏
• uninterested	❏	❏	❏
• uninteresting	❏	❏	❏
• unprofessional	❏	❏	❏
• unsure	❏	❏	❏
• untrustworthy	❏	❏	❏
• wasteful	❏	❏	❏

Those are not the most pleasant adjectives, but unfortunately, each of us knows someone who fits each dreadful descriptive. Let's be sure that person is not you. These negative attributes will block your ability to connect with others.

Consider yourself in the good times and the bad. Sometimes a person's mood will determine the image he projects at that moment. Although you may not normally be disrespectful and judgemental to others, if you've had a bad day and your patience has worn thin, you could find yourself rolling your eyes at an innocent bystander.

This happens to everyone at some point, but knowing your personal triggers that cause your "not-so-nice" behaviours is the first step needed to avoid unprofessional mishaps. Understanding the importance of how the image you portray affects your personal brand will hopefully motivate you to keep yourself in check.

MY MOST NEGATIVE DESCRIPTIVES

1 _____

2 _____

3 _____

4 _____

5 _____

Once you've completed a list of the descriptives that describe the reality of the Business of YOU, compare it to your ideal image list completed in the last chapter.

> **We all know someone who fits each dreadful descriptive. Let's be sure that person is not you.**

Now for the clincher: how far apart are your lists of descriptives, namely those you wish others would use to describe you and those they *do* use to describe you?

What are the consequences of portraying the image you currently portray? If you're rude and demanding at the dentist office, what happens if people in the waiting room overhear your comments? How would you appear if you treat your executive assistant inappropriately when your best client is nearby waiting to speak with you?

One by one, you can adjust your sails so everything moves together harmoniously. The idea of this exercise is not to become perfect, but to identify the potential idiosyncrasies that could hinder your ability to connect positively with others and keep others from connecting positively with you.

Recognizing shortcomings is just the beginning. Now, you'll need to take action to achieve your ideal personal image. Focus on one or two key descriptives to change at a time. Make a commitment to address one issue. Once you've overcome it, move to the next priority on your list.

MY COMMITMENTS FOR SELF-IMPROVEMENT

_____

_____

_____

_____

12 Why it Matters

In today's competitive world, you can't afford to let your competition be the one creating the mini-bonds with your current and potential clients. Solid relationships will help you maintain and gain clients in good times and when times are tough.

It's all about putting yourself in a position to win. As much as you may think optimizing your first impression and personal brand are superficial places to invest your time and financial resources, they can make or break you. It's the reality of human nature. You can either fight reality or you can make it work for you.

> **In today's competitive world, you can't afford to let your competition be the one creating the mini-bonds with your current and potential clients.**

Understanding the difference between your ideal image and your actual image is the first step needed to ensure your business networking success.

Even if you don't want to admit it, your competition, for the most part, delivers a quality product that is comparable to yours. You're probably thinking that's not true – you deliver a far superior product or service. That's good. That's what you should believe, BUT your average contact doesn't know that for sure.

To people looking for an accountant, every accountant is just another numbers person. An insurance advisor is just another person who sells insurance. A banker is just another banker. You and I know differently, but remember – a person's perception is his reality.

People will use your competition for many reasons. Perhaps they feel a stronger connection with them than they do with you. This could be through no fault of your own. Your competitors may have met them first and the relationship between them has longevity on its side or it could be that you haven't met them at all. If that's the case, how could you expect them to think to call you over your competition?

"

To earn a client's business, especially to take it away from your competition, you need to create a better bond and comfort level with the client than they have with your competition.

"

Or maybe, just maybe, your competitor makes a better impression than you.

Assuming you and your competition are competitive in product or service delivery, then the decision to choose to work with you over someone else is based primarily on emotion. It's the intangible reaction based on how much or how little you are liked, trusted and considered competent.

To earn a client's business, especially to take it away from your competition, you will need to create a better bond and comfort level with the client than they have with your competition. Ultimately, it's the relationship that will dictate where a person chooses to do business. The foundation for the relationship starts with the Business of YOU.

Whatever you project is what you will attract. Miserable people are magnets for others who will reinforce their misery. Similarly, those who are confident, happy and welcoming will generally be surrounded by people with similar qualities. Who do you think your clients and potential clients would prefer to do business with?

13 First Impressions

People start to form opinions of you the moment you meet. Regardless if your paths will cross for only a moment or if it's the beginning of a wildly successful business relationship, the first several seconds of interaction lay the groundwork for what's to come.

Although it may seem superficial, the reality is, it's the initial reaction that sticks. It may only take seconds to make a first impression, but it takes a lifetime to break one. It's important to invest in your outward image to maximize your opportunity to make a positive first impression.

There are several factors that contribute to the impression you make. Many of these are outlined in the following pages. Each, on its own, may not be the deal breaker, but combined, they will contribute to the gut reaction other people have about you.

14 Personal Hygiene and Grooming

The foundation of your image begins with the basics of personal hygiene and grooming. Those who look clean, smell pleasant and project a healthy, well-put-together image are more appealing than those who look and smell like they just rolled out of bed.

When you respect your own appearance, you will naturally seem more professional, confident and welcoming. What shows on the outside is a reflection of what you are on the inside.

> **What do you want your outward image to say about you as new contacts make snap first judgements?**

What do you want your outward image to say about you as new contacts make snap first judgements? The obvious day-to-day activities that lead to a well-polished image can get lost in the midst of juggling family, friends and career. Taking time for yourself on a daily, weekly and monthly basis is time well invested. Not only will you look better, you'll feel better too.

As young professionals, take an extra few minutes a day to create positive habits.

I often joke that they must not sell irons to people under the age of 25. An associate of mine who works in human resources can't believe the number of young interviewees who show up wearing wrinkled clothes.

Give yourself benchmarks for living. If an article of clothing has hit the floor or stayed in the dryer too long, unless it hits an ironing board first, it shouldn't enter the public domain.

Similarly, if you have to sniff a piece of clothing to determine its eligibility as a clean garment worthy of public presentation and you hesitate – that's a surefire sign that it isn't. Send it to the cleaners.

Wash your hands after using the facilities, for your own hygiene and the comfort of the next person whose hand you will shake.

Men and women should keep their nails manicured and clean. There is no shame in a man going for a manicure, and women, it's a great way to take a little breather in this hectic world. At the very least, men and women should use moisturizer. Rough hands are uncomfortable to shake. Nail biters, try to break your nasty habit. Yes, it is a difficult one to break, but it's an important one to conquer. Bitten nails and cuticles are noticeable.

Women, if you haven't changed your hairstyle in five years, assume you need a new look. A bad hair day can dampen the spirits of any woman and unkempt hair can detract from the most attractive and appropriate outfit. Hair is a significant part of a professional image. No matter what your hair's natural habits, texture or colour, with the right stylist and hair products you can generate a great hairstyle.

If you constantly struggle with your hair, find a new stylist. The best way to find a good stylist is to ask someone with similar hair-type and a great style where she gets her hair done and what products she uses. Be sure to tell the stylist who referred you so she has an opportunity to thank her walking billboard. Ask your hairdresser for tips on how to style your hair professionally at home, between cuts.

Fragrance should be kept to a minimum. There are so many people with allergies, you never know who could react unfavourably to your scent. A light scent is okay, except in fragrance-free zones. Anything that can be "appreciated" from more than a foot away is too much.

15 Professional Wardrobe

It's easy to rebel and suggest you don't really care what people think; therefore, you'll wear whatever you want to wear – that's your taste and it really doesn't matter. Well, actually, yes, it does matter.

Your clothes are the outside reflection of how you feel on the inside. In today's society, when people make snap judgements to decide if they are interested in getting to know you on a deeper level, the clothes you wear will be one determining factor in this decision.

That doesn't mean you need to head to the latest designer's store and blow your budget– quite the contrary. Professional wardrobes can be created on tight budgets. Plan to buy the best that you can afford.

> **Your clothes are the outside reflection of how you feel on the inside.**

Wardrobe development should be a proactive activity, not a reactive one. Start with what you have. Go through all of your clothes hanging in your closest. Do this with a professional style-conscious friend or an image consultant who knows and understands the image you want to portray.

Decide if each article of clothing adds to a professional image or detracts from it. Items that do not coincide with your ideal image should be given away, sold, perhaps through a consignment shop, or kept for social time.

Next, decide if the clothes in your professional pile are flattering to you. Do they fit well, match today's style and convey an appropriate message?

Once you know what you have that looks great, makes you feel good and presents a professional style, make a list of what's missing and shop accordingly. When you plan to buy clothes that are flattering, you can avoid knee-jerk shopping sprees that waste money on items that will not (or should not) leave your closet to see the light of day.

If you struggle with your wardrobe, invest in the services of a professional image consultant. The financial investment will save you a sizeable amount of money in the long run.

Here are some quick guidelines for men and women to use when developing a professional wardrobe.

WOMEN

Fewer quality pieces accessorized differently can expand your wardrobe substantially while keeping it current.

The more covered you are, the more professional you are perceived to be. Ask yourself, "If my husband or boyfriend were talking with a woman dressed like this, would I be comfortable?" If the answer is no, change. You have more to offer in the boardroom than your breasts, so keep them covered to keep men focussed on the task at hand – not where they may like to put their hands.

> **To judge if your skirt is too short, sit in a chair in front of a mirror and cross your legs.**

This applies for formal business events as well. Just because the invitation says black tie, this is not the time to bring out your swankiest, sexiest dress that will have all the men gawking.

Skirts should be an appropriate length. To judge if your skirt is too short, sit in a chair in front of a mirror and cross your legs. Can you see up your skirt? If so, how far? That should answer your question.

Nylons are more professional than bare legs. Many women complain about how uncomfortable nylons are, but really, even if they are sheer, your legs are still considered covered. Again, it comes down to knowing what image you want to portray. During hot months, wearing nylons to the office may not be necessary, but you should wear them to important business meetings and networking events.

You may have noticed that nylons do not repair themselves, so when they have a hole or run, throw them out rather than putting them back into your nylon drawer. This will save you a lot of time and frustration in the morning.

Solid colours are more professional than small prints and designs. Stronger fabrics send a stronger message. Well-tailored suits can still look feminine and sophisticated. The goal is not to look like a man, but to look like a credible professional.

Dark make-up is for when it is dark outside. Even if you're not a make-up person, add a little lip gloss and some mascara to add extra polish to your look. It sends a message that you care about yourself and took time to get ready.

MEN

Some would say men have it easy when it comes to dressing, but that's not always the case. Hopefully you either have a sense of style or a good tailor, woman or friend in your life to keep you matched and appropriately dressed.

Business-casual apparel equates to a button down shirt, a nice pair of slacks and a 'polishable' pair of shoes – not a t-shirt, a pair of jeans and sneakers. Golf shirts are technically casual. Offices with business-casual dress codes that inadvertently become everyday "casual" can send the wrong message to clients. It could say that you're lax on your deliverables.

Your socks should match or be darker than the hem of your pants. When you walk into a room with dark pants, dark shoes and white or tan socks, the bright socks are the first thing noticed. Your socks shouldn't walk into a room, you should.

Dark suits are less memorable than light ones. Therefore, you can get away with wearing the same navy suit every other day, but wearing a grey or light coloured suit regularly will make you known as the guy in the grey suit.

If an invitation requests business-formal or black tie attire, a dark suit is the minimum required. You will stick out as too casual if you wear a tan or grey jacket into a formal function. A tuxedo should be worn for black tie affairs.

Invest in quality tailored suits and add dynamics to your wardrobe with crisp and fashionable ties and shirts.

16 A Smile

"

A genuine smile will draw people to you.

"

Nothing is more uplifting and welcoming than a sincere, confident smile. Some people smile naturally; for others, getting them to smile is like pulling teeth.

If you are enjoying yourself, take a moment to notify your face so it can notify others. A genuine smile can set people at ease and invite others to talk with you.

Subconsciously, a smile communicates that you're confident, engaged, enjoying yourself, approachable, happy, and compelling – and that's just for starters.

A genuine smile will draw people to you. The next time you walk into a business function, look around the room. Whom would you prefer to talk with, the person who looks happy or the one who looks like she'll suck the energy right out of you? The difference between the two is usually a smile.

Those who are larger or more gruff looking by nature should take special note of their smile tendencies. Contacts may be intimidated by your sheer size and stature. A smile can help dispel any potential intimidation.

Not only can a smile affect how others perceive you, it's an easy way to adjust your own mood. When you don't feel like being around people or are unhappy, put a smile on your face and see how it changes your entire demeanour. Your subconscious won't know the difference.

> **"**
>
> **Not only can a smile affect how others perceive you, it's an easy way to adjust your own mood.**
>
> **"**

If you are self-conscious about your smile, figure out why. Would you be happier if you had your teeth bleached? Do you need dental work? A year of braces is less painful than a lifetime of hiding a smile.

17 Eye Contact

Eyes are the window to the soul. If you truly want to connect with others, give them this subconscious opportunity to see right into you. A person who constantly avoids eye contact insinuates shiftiness and/or a lack of interest or confidence.

Proper eye contact communicates that you are listening. Have you ever tried to talk with someone who is watching television? The TV watcher may hear what you are saying, but it's tough to believe he's really listening to you or caring about what you have to say.

To connect with someone, make and maintain eye contact, not in a phoney, stiff, hypnotic trance kind of way, but in a genuine, "I'm–only-focused-on-you–right-now" kind of way.

"

To connect with someone, make and maintain eye contact.

"

The most effective way to snub someone is to avoid eye contact when he is trying to talk with you. When you fail to genuinely acknowledge people with eye contact, they will get the loud and clear message that you're not interested in talking with them. If that's not the message you want to send, then make eye contact.

If possible, avoid wearing dark or mirrored sunglasses as they make it difficult for people to see your eyes.

A friend of mine quizzes his kids about people's eye colour after they interact with them. It's a great way to teach kids – and adults – about making eye contact. When was the last time you noticed a casual contact's eye colour?

Wandering eyes are the ultimate subliminal insult. Insincere politicians are notorious for this and so are people who are really not focused on you. The eyes wander when a person is not engaged in the conversation because he is actually scanning the room for the next, more important person. Even if that's not the intention, that's what wandering eyes communicate.

If you see someone in your peripheral vision and accidentally allow your eyes to wander (sometimes it just happens), simply acknowledge it. "Oh there's so and so. I was really hoping to catch up with him; do you know him too or shall I introduce you?" Or you could just open your entire body position to allow for the passer-by to enter the conversation. By acknowledging your wandering eyes, you will dispel any feeling of disinterest while making the person you were talking with in the first place feel like he is still in the loop.

18 Authenticity

By definition, you can't fake being authentic. You don't need to look in a dictionary to figure that out – it's easy to spot a phoney person.

They are obvious and usually not very well liked. Unfortunately, these are the same people who are so consumed with putting on airs that they don't realize others can see through their act.

It's the person who pretends to like you and then rolls his eyes as you turn away. Or the person who has a frown, followed by a huge fake smile that immediately fades when heads are turned. Or the person who offers an insincere compliment followed by an insincere invitation for lunch.

> **"**
>
> **Depending on the environment, your behaviour will change, but your core character should not.**
>
> **"**

Don't think for a moment the contact and/or others who are close by don't notice such unwelcoming, insincere behaviour. Genuinely happy interactions with people will elicit a smile that will naturally stay on your face even after the conversation is finished. Allow a smile to form and disappear at a natural, genuine pace.

Contacts will see through a façade eventually and really, putting on airs must be exhausting. At the end of the day, only you will know the real you. Not being true to yourself will hinder your ability to connect with others and, most importantly, keep you from being truly happy.

Consistency in character is essential to projecting an authentic image. If you treat everyone equally and stay true to your personal values and beliefs, this shouldn't be a challenge. Depending on the environment, your behaviour will change, but your personality and core character should not. The Business of YOU remains constant.

Keep compliments sincere, appropriate and gender neutral. The acceptable rule of thumb is that it's safe to compliment a woman's taste, but not her genetics.

> **"**
>
> **Keep compliments sincere, appropriate and gender neutral.**
>
> **"**

A lack of confidence or a feeling of inadequacy will cause professionals to pretend to be something they are not. Trying to figure out who everyone else wants you to be is impossible. Each person's opinion will be different.

When it comes to building your professional network, the best person you can be is you – authentically you.

19 Approachability

Body language tells tales – long, accurate tales.

Standing with your arms crossed and a scowl on your face does not make you seem inviting. Ignoring people around you to only focus on the 'important' people makes you seem snobby – and snobs are rarely liked, especially by other snobs.

Standing in a corner, moving quickly through a crowd, avoiding eye contact, turning your back to someone, looking others up and down and acting judgemental are all conscious or subconscious ways to tell contacts to stay away.

To project an approachable image, keep an open stance with arms uncrossed and a smile on your face. Look like you want to talk with others. Keep your eyes focused at eye level rather than looking to the ground, which is a surefire way to avoid engaging people. Slow down when you walk through a crowd to give people a chance to catch your attention.

Whenever possible, face the crowd rather than putting your back to people. Obviously, in crowded areas you're bound to have your back to someone, but particularly when someone is trying to catch your attention, position yourself to face that person.

For the most part, meeting strangers is an intimidating experience, particularly for those who are shy, so projecting a welcoming personality will set others at ease. The more comfortable you can make others feel, the more likeable you will be.

20 The Tone and Pitch of Your Voice

Chances are the tone and pitch of your voice are the last things you think about unless you're a professional speaker or singer. Most of us are not singers, but our voices still matter. How we sound affects how we are perceived.

For the average person, this is not a real challenge, but for some, an unpleasant voice can make it difficult to attract contacts who will like you, trust you and think you are competent.

I know there are times when I get really excited telling a story and my voice will become high-paced and high-pitched, making it difficult for others to understand what I'm saying. Being aware of this, I now take a deep breath and make a conscious effort to ensure my voice is comfortably audible and the pace of my speech is such that others can follow what I am saying. The content of my story may not change, but people's ability to understand it will.

To determine if you have nasty voice habits, your best bet, aside from recording yourself, is to notice others' reactions when you speak.

Do you speak too softly? This may very well be the case if people are always leaning towards you and squinting while you speak so they can

> **To determine if you have nasty voice habits, notice others' reactions when you speak.**

hear you better. If conversation partners seem to "tuneout" when you speak or are not engaging in the conversation, it may be that they simply can't hear you.

A soft speaking voice will make it difficult for people to hear you and can give others the impression that you are timid, insecure or hesitant. Using a firm, confident voice will present a much more professional image.

On the opposite end of the spectrum, do you speak too loudly? Do people several feet away always seem to be eavesdropping or looking at you as if your conversation is infringing on theirs?

A hearing loss may be the reason you speak so loudly, in which case, take appropriate action by getting your hearing tested. Once hearing loss is ruled out as the cause for your loud talking, simply follow the sound advice my big brother would tell me: "Take it down a notch."

Noisy speakers can be especially annoying in restaurants and at meetings. Have you ever sat beside someone who thinks he is whispering, but everyone turns to look at the two of you? It's especially annoying when a speaker is talking from a podium.

Another way to tell if you're too loud is to notice your conversation partner's body language. Are people constantly telling you to shush or looking around to see who may be overhearing you? A boisterous laugh can give the impression that you are immature, seeking attention, obnoxious or purposely allowing others to hear what you are saying.

Do you mumble or talk too quickly? The clarity of how you say something is as important as the volume at which you say it. Do others find it difficult to understand you? It is a good indication that this is the case if people routinely say, "Pardon?" or even worse, "What?" and ask you to repeat yourself. If so, make a serious effort to slow down and pronounce your words clearly.

When you are nervous, perhaps at the podium giving a speech or meeting someone you admire, the natural tendency is to speed up, so it's important to be mindful of your pace.

Most voice problems can be solved with some self-awareness and self-discipline. People with extreme voices can hire a voice coach to help them become more audibly pleasing.

21 A Sense of Humour

Sharing a laugh with someone is an excellent way to create a mini-bond. Laughing drops the defenses, has amazing physiological effects and can make a new contact seem like an old chum. A moment of true laughter can stem from a situation, a funny comment or a joke.

When it comes to jokes, it's a tough call. Some people can tell jokes; some people can't. It's important to acknowledge in which category you fit. If you're not sure, assume you can't.

There is a fine line between appropriate and inappropriate humour in business settings and unfortunately, as people become more familiar with contacts, the lines become even more blurred. When you are at a business function you should be acting in a professional capacity on behalf of your company. Know your audience and err on the side of caution to ensure you are presenting a positive, professional image at all times.

Once you've decided if a joke has appropriate content for your environment, determine if the length of the joke can survive the hustle and bustle of an event. Jokes that take longer than three sentences to complete are very difficult to deliver effectively.

Inevitably, someone will interrupt and you'll rarely get to the punch line. It's a common occurrence for people to restart the same joke to include newcomers or because people lost track of the plot. Unless the story is really engaging, you'll lose people because generally their attention spans are short.

Save inappropriate jokes for close friends in non-business settings. Running the risk of offending someone is not worth the laugh you may garner. Until you have a reasonable understanding of a contact's personality and particular sense of humour, anything that could be taken out of context is too risky.

Making fun of another person is never acceptable. It may have you laughing at the moment, but in the long-run your professionalism is shot. If you are heard making fun of someone as he walks away, it's only natural for the person who hears to wonder if you'll do the same thing when he leaves. Your like and trust factors are diminished.

Sexist comments or suggestive innuendos, although very common, are simply not appropriate.

22 Confidence

There were occasions, not too long ago, when I was so nervous talking in front of crowds that my voice would crack, my hands would shake and my face would turn bright red.

The worst was watching the faces in the crowd respond to my unease at the podium. Half were probably thankful they weren't addressing the crowd and the other half, I'm sure, were wondering who gave me a microphone. I can still remember the pained expression on one man's face as I introduced a political speaker – to this day I cringe whenever I think about it.

Then there were other times when I sounded like a professional. Cool, calm and collected as I charmed the crowd.

Finally I figured out the difference. It was preparation. When I knew exactly what I wanted to say and I stuck to my plan, I appeared confident because I was confident. Slowly, but surely, this idea helped me overcome my fear of public speaking. Whenever I had to speak, I'd set aside time to prepare notes and I'd be all set.

> **Developing confidence has been the single most important personal transformation that has affected my career.**

Thank goodness I figured that out; otherwise running for political office and launching a professional speaking career would not have been possible.

The same scenario was true for me with events. At times I would walk into a room and feel like a fish out of water, while other times I felt like a part of the crowd. This was because I lacked confidence. Overcoming this was not an easy task.

For me it took several years of stretching my comfort zone to find true confidence, but it was well worth it. From my perspective, developing confidence has been the single most important personal transformation that has affected my career.

> **Confidence, or what I interpret as being comfortable in your own skin, will set others at ease.**

It's important to find the sensitive balance between confidence and a flashing ego. Confidence, or what I interpret as being comfortable in your own skin, will set others at ease. You will exude welcoming qualities and people will see you as someone who has it together.

A healthy dose of ego can have the same benefits, but displaying too much ego can annoy people, repel them and make them feel substandard. Ironically, projecting an intense ego or an extraordinarily high opinion of self usually masks a secret lack of self-confidence – so don't be too intimidated by the pompous folks in the crowd.

People are naturally drawn to confident people. Those who radiate confidence have that certain charisma about them that is usually followed by success.

A lack of confidence can be misinterpreted as non-interest and/or inapproachability when actually, the problem is that you're just feeling out of your element.

> **"**
>
> **True confidence allows you to take your eyes off yourself and focus on other people.**
>
> **"**

True confidence allows you to take your eyes off yourself and focus on other people. Confidence lets you take risks. It keeps you from second guessing your every move. I remember years ago hearing a speaker who said, 'There is the speech you're going to give, the one you give to the crowd and the one you give to your steering wheel on the way home.'

That's what my entire life felt like. I would meet someone and then replay in my head over and over again all of the stupid things I said during our conversations. It would drive me crazy. I spent more time worrying than actually enjoying the moment. Perhaps you can relate.

Finally I came to the conclusion that I had to deal with my confidence issues once and for all. I was not prepared to spend my life living in the shadow of some fictitious perfect image I constantly strived to be rather than accepting who I truly was.

Without confidence, it's difficult to connect with other professionals. Time spent worrying is time that could be used to build relationships.

There's a difference between not having self-confidence and being nervous about stretching your comfort zone. It's normal to be uneasy about taking the next steps as you build your business network. Walking into a room filled with strangers could cause the most confident professionals to hesitate.

Just recently I was in another city at a function where I knew I'd only know a few of the expected guests. I was early; all of my friends were late. This left me gulping for air in unfamiliar territory. It had been a long time since I had that sinking feeling of, "Oh my goodness, who will I talk with?" My first instinct was to wait in the car until the people I knew arrived. Then, I remembered my own advice, got out of my car, stood up straight, put a smile on my face and walked into a room full of people I did not know – yet.

My first conversation was with one of the organizers at the reception desk. I genuinely congratulated her on what seemed to be a successful event judging by the number of people in the room. (The people at the registration table are always safe bets if you're looking for conversation partners to break the ice. However, don't talk with them for too long because they will have others to welcome to the event.)

Next, I made my way to the bar. Then, with drink in hand, I noticed a group talking nearby. I made eye contact with one of the members of the group. This allowed me to walk over and say hello. By the time my associates arrived I'd already met several people and had three new business cards. I would have missed these opportunities if I had opted to wait in the car for my friends.

23 Developing Networking Confidence

Those of you who are truly confident, feel free to skip to the next section. However, it's my experience that all of us can use a little boost in our self-confidence in order to enhance our networking skills, so you may wish to keep reading this chapter.

Looking back on my personal journey, I know there were three key elements that drastically affected my confidence level. They are the same three words that were referenced earlier as important to building your ultimate network.

PERSPECTIVE, PREPARATION, AND PRACTICE

To build confidence, you need to change your **perspective** on matters that influence your confidence. Once you grasp a few simple realities of human nature, it's easier to gain perspective and become comfortable in the networking world.

The greatest realization for me was that most of my fears weren't warranted. Even when embarrassing moments happened or when I thought I made a less-than-stellar impression, I still managed to function and found that more often than not, most people didn't notice my fauxpas at the time or if they did, didn't remember it after the fact.

You'll find aspects of **preparation** throughout this entire book. Dealing with the Business of YOU, developing a solid professional image, mastering the fundamentals and having a proactive strategy are all parts of preparation. By dealing with these up front, you will be confident that you are making a great first impression, allowing you to take your eyes off yourself and focus on others.

Next, confidence takes **practice**. The more business networking you experience, the easier it will be and the more confident you will become. Genuine confidence will give your business networking efforts a sense of ease and allow you to enjoy the process. By continually challenging yourself to poke through the top of your comfort zone, you will eventually recreate and elevate your comfort zone boundaries.

The concepts presented in this book, when implemented, will make a significant impact on your business confidence, allowing you to genuinely connect with others to build your ultimate network. Confidence takes time to build, so be patient with yourself.

24 Seven Steps to Elevated Confidence

1   IDENTIFY YOUR VALUE-ADDED QUALITIES

2   IDENTIFY YOUR FEARS AND CONFIDENCE ZAPPERS

3   IMAGINE THE WORST CASE SCENARIOS

4   FIX IT OR ACCEPT IT

5   STOP APOLOGIZING

6   TAKE YOUR EYES OFF YOU

7   MAKE IT HAPPEN

STEP 1: IDENTIFY YOUR VALUE-ADDED QUALITIES

The first step to developing confidence is to understand why you deserve to be confident. What valuable qualities do you bring to relationships? What do you offer that could benefit others and make them want to know you?

What makes you great? What benefits come with knowing you? What makes you special? Why do you think your friends are your friends? What are your strengths? Why would someone be lucky to know you? Don't be shy. This list is for your eyes only.

When you make your list, don't focus on superficial attributes. If the best you can write about yourself is that you have good hair, one bad hair day and your confidence is sure to fall flat.

> *Write down all of your positive qualities – don't stop until you hit a minimum of 20.*

20 REASONS I'M A WONDERFUL PERSON

1 _____

2 _____

3 _____

4 _____

5 _____

6 _____

7 _____

8 _____

9 _____

10 _____

11 _____

12 _____

13 _____

14 _____

15 _____

16 _____

17 _____

18 _____

19 _____

20 _____

> *Every morning read the list as soon as you wake up.*
> ***Internalize it. Believe it. Exude it.***

STEP 2: IDENTIFY YOUR FEARS AND CONFIDENCE ZAPPERS

Write down all your fears and confidence zappers in the first column on the Confidence Chart on Page 70. What do you not like about yourself that makes you feel unworthy? Are you afraid you'll say something stupid? Are you concerned you'll trip and fall flat on your face? Do you fear people will laugh at you? Do you worry you don't have enough education or that you're not good enough? Are you unhappy with your image and feel others won't like you?

Do you even know why you lack confidence? It's impossible to develop confidence until you understand why you don't have it in the first place.

> *In this step, do some real soul searching and decide exactly what it is that keeps you from feeling truly confident. What expectations do you have for yourself? Where do you feel you fall short? If you feel you don't belong, why? Write it ALL down. Be honest with yourself. Again, this is for your eyes only.*

STEP 3: IMAGINE THE WORST CASE SCENARIO

What if your biggest fears became realities? What are the consequences if the worst case scenarios were true?

> Let your imagination roam as you take every fear and confidence zapper and play the scenarios out in your mind. Write them down in the Confidence Chart on Page 70.

"

Are your confidence zappers legitimate reasons for people to not like you or for you to feel out of place?

"

What if you said something stupid? What would that stupid thing be? What if you fell flat on your face? What if people laughed at you? What if you don't have enough education? What if you're not good enough? How will your life be impacted if the worst case scenario happened to you?

Now ask yourself, how likely is the worst case scenario to happen? Are your confidence zappers legitimate reasons for people to not like you or for you to feel out of place? Consider people you know. Can you think of anyone who has experienced the very things that worry you? How were they affected? Are they still liked by others or were their reputations ruined?

Chances are it'll be difficult to find anyone who has actually suffered and not recovered from the very concerns that keep you from living a confident life. Accept that your fears are unlikely to come true and if they do, accept that they are usually not the issues that will impact others' opinions of you. This will allow you to stop worrying about the fictional worst-case scenarios and focus on connecting.

Review this list again in 24 hours. Time will give you some perspective on the worst-case scenarios and their likelihood of ever occurring or impacting your life. Hopefully once you reread your comments, you'll find, as I did, that things are rarely as bad as they seem at first glance.

> *Record your new 24 hour perspectives on Page 70.*
> *Are your fears really warranted?*

STEP 4: FIX IT OR ACCEPT IT

Now that we've identified what's holding you back we need to get you out of your own way so you can build your ultimate network. To do this, you have two options to develop confidence: either fix your concerns or accept them.

What keeps us from having true confidence is our inability to fix or accept our shortcomings and ignore unjustifiable fears. This enables these perceived inadequacies and worries to hold us back from achieving optimal success.

In steps two and three, you made a list of all the barriers that keep you from feeling truly confident. To truly overcome your personal hurdles, you need to find your own solutions. Look at each challenge individually.

"

What keeps us from having true confidence is our inability to fix or accept our shortcomings and ignore unjustifiable fears. This enables these perceived inadequacies and worries to hold us back from achieving optimal success.

"

Are you willing to accept the consequences of the worst-case scenario if it happened? If not, do you have the courage, attitude and commitment needed to fix the very confidence zappers that keep you from connecting with others?

There are some things about ourselves that we can't fix, leaving acceptance as the only choice. For each item that you've identified as a confidence zapper, decide if you can fix it and if not, how you can accept it and move forward.

What advice would you give your best friend to deal with these potential challenges and fears? Now, as difficult as it may be, it's time to take your own advice.

For example, if one of your confidence zappers is that you don't feel that you dress professionally enough to be taken seriously, that's an easy one to fix. Find a friend who has a professional style. The two of you can go through your closet and pull together outfits that are professional and ones that are not. Mix and match different suits and accessories so you have several different outfits (even if they come from a few basic pieces). Having professional outfits organized in advance will give you confidence and make it easier to get ready in the morning. Problem solved.

Other confidence-zappers aren't as easy to fix. This is where perspective is so important. Do you really think people will like you less because of your height or weight, a speech impediment or your substandard car? Likely not. Most people are too busy worrying about themselves to worry about what qualities and possessions you do or do not have.

If something is of specific concern to you, ask yourself, "How can I divert focus from my shortcomings so people see my strengths?"

There are normal risks to life, like the potential to fall down in front of a crowd and/or to say something stupid, but you can't let those fears hold you back from having huge success. I always figure, minimize the risk and have faith that you can recover from those less-than-impressive moments. (Refer to Chapter 25 on Recovery.)

> *Decide for each confidence zapper whether you will accept it or fix it and record your action plans on Page 70.*

STEP 5: STOP APOLOGIZING

The best way to zap your confidence is to continually apologize for your shortcomings. It keeps you from focusing on your strengths. Catch your negative self-talk.

For every negative comment you make about yourself, contradict it with two positive thoughts.

It's an excellent habit to develop that will eventually change your perspective about yourself.

If you've ever said or felt that you don't want to waste someone's time by talking with him, you have a confidence problem. It is not average behaviour to apologize for communicating with someone. I hear people say it all the time: "I don't want to bother you...but...can you...?"

Truly successful people are not "bothered" by people talking with them. They become "bothered" when someone does something that is bothersome, like pointing out you are bothering them. Your existence is not 'bothersome.' Saying please and thank you are enough words when asking for input or a favour.

"

For every negative comment you make about yourself, contradict it with two positive thoughts.

"

STEP 6: TAKE YOUR EYES OFF YOU

Be conscious of yourself, not self-conscious.

Deal with the Business of YOU. Accept or fix your confidence zappers so you can focus on other people and their needs. Take a genuine interest in others and adopt a "pay it forward" attitude. Always ask yourself, "What can I offer this person besides the product I sell? How can I make someone else's day better? What can I do to help others?" Good deeds have a way of boomeranging out of the blue.

When you take your eyes off yourself, you will be less likely to feel self-conscious. This will free you to embrace potential business relationship opportunities and friendships that are staring you in the face. The simple act of genuinely listening to a person can make the difference of whether or not a person feels valued when he's around you. If you make others feel valued, in turn you will be happier.

"

Be conscious of yourself, not self-conscious.

"

The most successful people are usually the most down to earth. We all put our pants on one leg at a time. It may be a cliché, but it's the truth. We all have feelings, fears, wants and needs. Everyone wants to belong. That's part of life. When we put other people on pedestals, no wonder it's difficult to connect with them – they're too far out of reach. It's only natural to feel self-conscious or intimidated by them if you hold them to such high standards. At the end of the day, people are just people.

> **Before you go into a function, review your list of 20 reasons why others would be fortunate to connect with you.**

If another person is at a business function, you already have something in common. You've both gone to the same place. Everyone in the room is there to meet new people and reconnect with current contacts. If they didn't want to interact with people, they would have stayed home.

Before you go into a function, review your list of 20 reasons why others would be fortunate to connect with you. This exercise will give you a last-minute confidence boost.

STEP 7: MAKE IT HAPPEN

The best way to expand your comfort zone is to give yourself mini-challenges. Encourage yourself (okay, force yourself if need be) to do things at the top edge or outside of your comfort zone. Sometimes you've just got to get out of your own way to let something happen. When you survive big or even small leaps of faith, you slowly, but surely, gain confidence.

Remember when you were a kid and you would get scared in the middle of the night? Then you would start playing that 1-2-3-go counting game over and over until you finally got the nerve to run to your parents' room.

When you finally ran through the house to safety, you were relieved the boogeyman missed you, at least for that night. Gradually, you overcame your fear and understood that the boogeyman doesn't exist. Then, instead of wasting all that valuable sleep time worrying about fictional worst-case scenarios, when you woke up from a nightmare, you'd just shake it off and go back to sleep.

Mastering events and interacting with other professionals can be tackled in the same way. Sometimes you just have to make it happen and trust that the "boogeyman", or your "confidence zapper" is a non-issue.

Until you truly feel confident, the best bet is to straighten your back, get dressed in your best outfit and put a smile on your face. To others you will appear confident and surprisingly, acting confidently will help you feel more confident. Your subconscious doesn't have a sense of humour so it won't know the difference.

> **"**
>
> **Until you truly feel confident, the best bet is to straighten your back, get dressed in your best outfit and put a smile on your face.**
>
> **"**

CONFIDENCE CHART

CONFIDENCE ZAPPER	WORST CASE SCENARIO	24 HOUR PERSPECTIVE	FIX IT / ACCEPT IT	ACTION PLANS TO OVERCOME

25 Recovering from Embarrassing Situations

Now that you've identified the biggest fears that zap your confidence, I need to tell you that sometimes embarrassing moments do happen and things can go wrong.

This fact shouldn't shake your confidence or keep you from getting out there and making things happen. As you interact with more and more people, unavoidable embarrassing moments are bound to happen.

How you react and recover in these times of tribulation will affect how others perceive you.

For example, if a waiter spills food all over your suit, you have two options. You can accept it, wipe yourself clean and make some refreshingly comical remark to make the waiter feel comfortable.

Or you can freak out, give the waiter hell, call the manager over to the table, demand dry cleaning money and stomp out of the restaurant as if you are the only person who has ever had food spilt on a suit.

I've witnessed both extremes. The first option makes you a much more likeable person. Food will come clean – your reputation as someone who overreacts while making others squirm may not.

After I had volunteered politically, an associate suggested I run for the party's provincial executive. I was still getting my feet wet in these political circles. I knew it could be a rewarding experience because I'd grown up around politics, so I stretched my comfort zone and accepted the challenge.

Not long after, the soon-to-be-president of the executive was hosting his campaign launch party in Toronto. It was a perfect opportunity for me to meet the "big-wigs" of the party in hopes of winning their support.

Before I started mingling, I went upstairs to use the restroom. Upon my return, I paused at the top of the stairs to get a feel for the room below. I made eye contact with a group of gentlemen at the bottom of the long staircase. Knowing full well these were the go-to guys I needed to impress and that all eyes were on me, I ever so confidently began my descent into the packed restaurant while maintaining eye contact with the group.

About halfway down the stairs, I discovered my strappy silver sandals were not the sturdiest footwear choice for a sweaty summer day and down I went – all the way to the bottom. I will never forget the look of horror on the gentlemen's faces as I bounced my way to ground level.

The momentum propelled me into the group. Perched on the leg that still had feeling, I offered a one-legged half-curtsey as I extended my arm to shake each hand. As if nothing happened, save of course, the dripping blood, I said, "Hi, Allison Graham. Nice to meet you."

Needless to say, my "graceful" entrance helped me win the election to the provincial executive. Later I was told the guys weren't sure they would support my nomination because they hadn't worked with me yet, but they figured anyone who could recover so graciously and quickly from such an entrance was destined to be in politics.

"

Good can come from bad situations when you look for the silver lining.

"

Yes, I could have made a u-turn, run upstairs and called it quits after embarrassing myself so publicly. Thankfully I didn't because in the end, the accident worked out in my favour. Good can come from bad situations when you look for the silver lining.

As you build your network, expect to be caught off guard. A sense of humour and the ability to laugh at yourself can be an endearing quality and will help people relate to you. It's impossible to relate to "perfect" people. Plus, knowing that you can recover from whatever life throws at you will take away pressure to be perfect and add a sense of confidence to your demeanour.

If becoming a mishap recovery specialist doesn't appeal to your personality, then feel confident knowing that most people won't even notice when you embarrass yourself and if they do, they won't care.

Aside from the gentlemen who later ran my campaign for the executive, I doubt any of the 400 people in the room have any recollection of my disastrous fall seven years ago. The only reason I guess the guys might remember vaguely is because my entrance became an entertaining topic while we worked on my campaign.

If you did something wrong or said something you wish you could take back, learn from the experience and avoid making the same mistake again next time.

When bad things happen, it's natural to replay your regrettable moments in your head. Reliving your not-so-fine blunders then beating yourself up doesn't help you build your network. Doing this can drive you batty and keep you from putting yourself out there. In these situations, I find it helpful to write about the embarrassing moments in my journal. Playing it out "officially" seems to bring perspective, as does time.

Think back on your professional career. What were your most embarrassing moments? How did you recover? Did those situations affect you profoundly? Was there anything positive that came out of the experiences? Were you ruined? Probably not.

MY MOST EMBARRASSING MOMENTS

_____

_____

_____

_____

THE RULES OF RECOVERY

1 If an embarrassing situation arises and it's accidental, do your best to find humour in the situation and go with the flow.

2 If you've done something wrong, recognize it, admit it, apologize appropriately and move on. Avoid gushing or over-apologizing because you run the risk of making the scenario worse and drawing negative attention to yourself.

3 If the situation is the fault of someone else, accept the apology and cut him some slack. Your easygoing nature and forgiving approach will add to your appeal both as a person and as a professional.

4 If you notice someone having an embarrassing moment, try to distract from the situation and/or find a way to save him. He'll be eternally grateful. To connect with others, you want them to feel comfortable around you. When a person has done something wrong or feels embarrassed, that's an opportunity for you to be the bigger person by setting him at ease.

26 Building Your Reputation

Once you're known, you'll be known for something. It's up to you to decide if that's a good or a bad reality. A positive reputation has the potential to open unlimited doors for you while a negative one can close them quickly.

The first step to consciously building your reputation is to determine if you are in fact trustworthy or competent. Convincing others of something that is not true won't last long, if it happens at all. If you determine that you aren't trustworthy or competent, then you're going to need more than this book to help you.

For the purposes of the concepts in this book, let's assume that you are both a trustworthy business person and you are more than capable of delivering a quality product and/or service.

> **"**
>
> **Your reputation, developed over time, will determine whether people trust you and think you are competent.**
>
> **"**

Every interaction with contacts will add to, reinforce or subtract from the opinion others have of you. Over time situations will arise where contacts will hear about you and interact with you. Each occurrence contributes to a deeper consideration of your existence, which ultimately equates to your reputation.

Mastering a positive first impression and being conscious of how you make others feel when they are around you will affect whether or not people like you. Your reputation, developed over time, will determine whether people trust you and think you are competent.

Have you ever heard someone say, "I wouldn't trust him as far as I could throw him"? That's a perfect example of a person's reputation being communicated. What are the chances you will choose to do business with that person?

As you expand your business network, you can't expect everyone will like you and sing your praises at every available moment – that's not a realistic expectation. However, there is a distinction between disliking someone because personalities clash and believing and actively sharing that a person's core character is flawed.

> **"**
>
> **Once you're known, you'll be known for something. It's up to you to decide if that's a good or a bad reality.**
>
> **"**

Time is your best ally in developing your reputation. If your ultimate goal is to be seen as a mover and shaker in your industry, then you need to know this will not happen in an instant. Chances are, there are already movers and shakers in your industry. Not only do you need to create a name for yourself, but also you'll need to earn your stripes.

Once you get noticed and expand your circles of influence, others inside and outside of your industry will take a more objective look at who you are, what you do and what you have to offer before you'll settle into your place within the industry's natural structure.

The keys to a positive reputation are to under-promise and over-deliver. If you exceed expectations you will be perceived as a real go-getter who is true to your word.

> **"**
>
> **There is a distinction between disliking someone because personalities clash and believing and actively sharing that a person's core character is flawed.**
>
> **"**

Repeatedly, people – especially young, naive professionals – get caught making unrealistic promises to make themselves sound important. Then, when push comes to shove, they can't deliver. When they drop the ball, inevitably someone has to pick it up and that major blunder can detract from the very essence of the professional image they're trying to achieve.

If you find yourself in over your head, the best approach is to come clean. No one minds if a committee member can't sell five tables to a charity ball. That's understandable. However, you lose friends and influence when you break such news to the gala organizer 24 hours before the event by returning 50 unsold tickets.

No one expects you to be Wonder Woman or Superman. They do expect you to do what you say you're going to do.

This rule applies to the small things as well. If you say casually, "I'll send you her contact details," make sure that when you return to your office, you actually send the contact details. Most of the time people just spew random comments like, "I'll get that information to you" or "I'll tell so and so to call you," then never follow through on their promises.

How many promised lunches do you have rolling around in the universe that you know will never happen? Unless you truly want to have lunch with a person, don't bother making the suggestion and running the risk of losing your credibility.

"Let's do lunch" statements flood the airwaves of business networking functions daily and yet, these invitations rarely materialize into real meetings. Each time you make false promises, this insincere behaviour chips away at your credibility and ruins your reputation.

> **"**
>
> **The keys to a positive reputation are to under-promise and over-deliver.**
>
> **"**

It's just as respectable to say, "I'll call you to discuss it" or "Why don't I pop by your office for 15 minutes for a coffee?" rather than committing to a meal or a golf game or any other activity in which you don't intend to partake.

Consistency is another major contributor to building trust and a positive reputation. A newbie networker who flashes onto the scene for two weeks and then disappears for six months makes it difficult for others to find him credible. Sure, sometimes life happens and you get busy; however, building your network is either a priority for you or it isn't. You make the call. It does less damage to do nothing than to start and stop over and over again.

That doesn't mean you need to be out networking seven nights a week, twelve months a year. When your to-do list is overloaded and you simply can't focus on building your network, it's important to maintain it. Take one hour each week to touch base with key contacts via telephone so they know you haven't dropped off the face of the earth.

Proving you're competent comes by doing – and doing well. Commit to delivering good service and over time your reputation will be that you do just that. Positive word of mouth buzz will be created and then everyone will want to work with you.

There is nothing that can damage a budding business relationship faster than failing to deliver when a person recommends you to a contact. Connecting people, especially for the first time, is a giant leap of faith. Inevitably the person who makes the referral feels responsible until the project is completed and completed well. If you fail to deliver as promised, you will lose your new client and your referral source.

In business, sometimes things go wrong. Everyone knows and accepts that. It's how you handle the mishaps that make all the difference as you develop your reputation. Open and honest communication is the best way to salvage potential blow-ups. Implement a personal service recovery model for when things go wrong.

Once you have a reputation built and are seen as a go-to person for your industry, maintaining your positive reputation requires that you stay the course: provide competent service, stay true to your word and remain visible.

"

Each time you make false promises, this insincere behaviour chips away at your credibility and ruins your reputation.

"

↗ Section 2 Summary

- A corporate brand is really the sum of all the personal brands that represent it. You can't control how people feel about you, you can only influence their perception of you by projecting a positive image.

- A good reputation is a powerful asset as you build your ultimate network. Do everything you can to earn and protect a positive reputation.

- Determine what image you want to portray so you can strive to achieve your ideal personal brand.

- No one expects you to be "ON" all the time, but when you're in public, ON is best and "Neutral" is the minimum standard. It's too risky to be "OFF" in public – you never know who's watching you.

- Today in business, age barriers are essentially non-existent. Personality, perception and performance count much more than age.

- Be conscious of yourself, not self-conscious.

- We're human, so no one is perfect. As a result, mistakes, accidents and blunders happen. Recognize when you've made a mistake and know the rules of recovery.

- Sharing a laugh can strengthen a bond. Be sure jokes and comments are appropriate for your audience.

- How you say something is as important as what you say. Be aware of the tone and pitch of your voice.

- Most confidence zappers are imaginary threats. We have the power to get a grip on ourselves and gain control so we are free to become the self-confident individuals we have a right to be.

Section 3
The Fundamentals

27 The Fundamentals

M astering the fundamentals of networking will give you a strong foundation on which to build your professional network. In some cases these may seem like obvious minor details, but in actual fact it's the little things that can make all the difference as you connect with others. The good news is that the fundamentals are easy to learn.

As we go through school and start our careers, the focus is on learning the specific skills required for our industry rather than learning the simple things that make life easy and give us the extra edge professionally.

As you read this section you may discover you've missed the mark on one or more of these skills. Even if you've been doing all of them wrong before reading this book, don't worry – you're in very good company. I've witnessed countless senior-level executives fumble with the fundamentals.

Learning these fundamental skills will help you focus on connecting with others rather than worrying about what fork to use or on which side of your body to put your name tag. With a little practice these skills will become automatic and give you a confidence boost because you won't have to second guess your every move.

Once you've mastered these skills, don't expect people to "ooh" and "ah" from across a crowded room. Actually, most people won't even notice when you're doing something right. The specifics will become non-issues.

When you mess up and do something wrong, that's when people in-the-know will notice.

If you master these fundamentals, you will, however, exude confidence and present a positive, professional image. Even if it's on a subconscious level, people will notice thatyou seem to have it "together," which will positively contribute to youroverall personal brand.

Keep in mind these ideas reflect North American traditions and when visiting other cultures you are encouraged to learn the best practices for those settings.

28 Handshakes

It's remarkable that in a professional networking book, I would have to tackle such a seemingly basic form of communication, but unfortunately, I've received enough bad handshakes to know it's a top priority.

A handshake is the subconscious communication of your character.

What does your handshake say about you? Does it give the impression that you are disinterested, unsure, unprofessional, overbearing, controlling, wishy–washy or insincere? Is your handshake solid, floppy, hurried, painful, blasé?

> **A handshake is the subconscious communication of your character.**

The ideal handshake joins two hands for a firm, web-to-web grip for two or three pumps and is then released. Your wrist is kept strong. Eye contact is imperative during this entire process: it completes the communication.

Yet so often, eye contact is missing altogether or it lasts for a mere half-second before you or your shaking partner look somewhere else. When I meet someone who doesn't look me in the eye when shaking my hand, I want to grab his chin and shift his head back front and centre to me and say, "Hello, yoo-hoo, we're in the middle of something here...if you are too important or uninterested to connect with me for under 10 seconds, why did you shake my hand in the first place?"

There are probably many reasons at the root of this lack of eye contact epidemic, but I'm not a psychologist. I'm just someone who has shaken a lot of hands. For some it may be a lack of confidence, or most likely, people just aren't aware they're not fully engaging in the handshake.

Create a mental trigger so that when you touch a person's hand for a handshake, you automatically look him in the eye.

Take special notice of eye contact (or the lack of it) in group situations. This is where professionals often fall short, even those who are good at making eye contact during single handshake introductions. There is a false sense of urgency to meet and greet when others are waiting their turn for an introduction. Rather than focusing on each individual, the greeter feels compelled to take a sneak peek at the next hand he is about to shake. Greet each person in a group dynamic as you would in a one-on-one setting.

Eye contact will increase your ability to connect with the other person. Make a conscious effort to make eye contact on your next opportunity to shake someone's hand and notice the difference.

As a professional in North America, one must accept that it is customary to shake hands. If you have a cold or are extremely germ phobic, simply deny the handshake, citing that you want to protect the other person from getting whatever illness you have.

At a recent conference, a colleague told me the story of how, immediately after shaking a new contact's hand, the gentleman pulled out a sanitizer bottle and used it right in front of him while they were still talking. How insulting! That's completely unacceptable.

I've not kept an official tally, but I would suggest about 50% of handshakes miss the mark on total professionalism. So basically, there is a 50/50 chance that you are a good hand shaker. Those aren't great odds. So let's tip the scale in your favour. To do that, we'll first take a look at some classic handshaking mistakes people make.

THE FLOPPY-FISH HANDSHAKE

This handshake speaks for itself. There's just no life to it. It's wimpy and weak. It has no "oomph." It communicates a lack of confidence, a sense of intimidation and/or a general uncertainty.

This is probably the most common handshake mistake. That's not surprising because many people lack confidence, are intimidated by others and are generally uncertain. On one hand (pardon the pun), this uncertainty could be the case. On the other hand, a floppy fish could indicate that someone is lazy and/or doesn't care about the introduction being made. Thus, it could also be called the "I-have-to-but-don't-want-to" handshake.

To overcome the floppy fish, just "buck up" and bring some life to your handshake. Keep your wrist strong. The floppy fish solution may be as simple as just realizing the importance of this form of communication. At the very least, even if you're crumbling inside from nervousness, offering a solid handshake won't make it so obvious to the person you are greeting.

THE CHURCH LADY HANDSHAKE

During this shake the person adds an extra hand to the mix and covers the top or side of the shaking hands. This is tricky to analyse. In some cases, it conveys sympathy and can create a deeper bond between people. For instance, this handshake is quite commonly used when meeting grieving family members in a receiving line at a funeral home. In this case, the handshake shows genuine concern and support.

However, if this handshake is used in a boardroom situation or during a business function when greeting another professional, it can be seen as an intimidation technique or construed as inappropriate touching. It's taking liberties to touch the top or side of another's hand.

This handshake should be reserved for close friends and associates in situations where you're actually showing sympathy and/or for little old church ladies.

THE SOAKER HANDSHAKE

It's never comfortable to receive a wet handshake. Usually, this problem is caused when you hold a cold drink glass, your hands sweat or you don't dry your hands completely after visiting the facilities.

To keep your hand dry, hold your drink in your left hand at cocktail receptions. If your hands sweat a lot, keep a napkin in your pocket so you can inconspicuously dry the hand you shake with before you use it for that purpose. If you don't have a pocket, keep a napkin cupped in your hand and switch the napkin to your left one just before you shake someone's hand. Take an extra moment to ensure your hands are completely dry after washing them.

THE BONE-CRUSHER HANDSHAKE

We've all been on the receiving end of one of these handshakes. There is a fine line between a solid grip and a painful squeeze. If you happen to notice people flinch when you shake hands with them or if you regularly find yourself in a testosterone-induced shaking battle, you are probably using too strong a grip. It could mean you're extra strong or you're trying to exhibit power. Bone crushers, please lighten your grip.

To save yourself from the pain of a bone crusher, simply split your "peace" fingers and place them on the crusher's wrist rather than cupping your fingers around the crusher's hand. It will keep your bones from grinding together. (Call it lessons learned thanks to an older brother.)

THE FINGER-LICKER HANDSHAKE

The completely unacceptable finger-licking shake happens far too often. It occurs when a person eating hors d'oeuvres at a cocktail party is kind enough to clean crumbs or grease from his fingers by licking all of them before shaking your hand. Don't laugh – yes, you may squirm – but this habit does exist. It's awkward to see a freshly licked hand coming towards you for a handshake. That's what napkins are for.

TEST YOUR HANDSHAKE

Not sure if you have a good handshake? Watch others' facial expressions when they shake your hand. Does it change? Do they look disappointed?

Ask a friend to test your handshake. The best handshake happens when you are testing because you're cognizant of how a handshake should be. Use this opportunity to consciously improve your grip. You really want to know if you have a strong handshake when you're meeting new contacts.

Therefore, it's a good idea to ask your friend to test you in a business setting when you're not thinking about being tested. That handshake is the one that counts and will give you real feedback.

Recently I introduced two colleagues to each other. They shook hands, said hello and we were on our way. Afterward, my friend commented on the "floppy-fish" she just received.

The next time I saw my "floppy-fish" contact was during a training session. When I talked about appropriate handshakes, I tested this person's handshake in front of the crowd – it was a perfect grip. When he wasn't paying attention to his handshake, it was a total flop.

HUGS

Hugs imply a sense of familiarity and thus should be kept for close friends and colleagues. To avoid a hug, simply offer your hand for a handshake instead. Hugs used as a greeting do not require tight or prolonged squeezes. Before going in for a hug, be sure the relationship you have with the other individual elicits one.

Offering one, two, or three "cheeky-air-kisses" is not a North American custom. It can make some feel uncomfortable and can be awkward, especially for those who don't wish to get up close and personal. To avoid the air kisses, simply extend your hand for the handshake and lock your elbow to keep your greeting partner at an acceptable distance.

29 Name Tags

You don't wear a name tag so people know what to call you; it's worn so people know who you are.

Names tags should include your first and last names plus your company name, all printed clearly. The power of a name tag is generally underestimated. A name tag is a cheat note posted on your chest for the benefit of others.

Considering the difficulty people have remembering names, using name tags properly can make it easier for people to figure out who you are and put you into context.

> **"**
>
> **You don't wear a name tag so people know what to call you; it's worn so people know who you are.**
>
> **"**

Placement of the name tag is equally as important as the information on it. Name tags should be placed high on your right shoulder, approximately three fingerwidths down from your collar bone.

Right-handed people tend to put their name tag on their left side because when the right elbow is bent, it naturally aligns to the left side. In actual fact, the name tag should be placed on your right shoulder. It's a little awkward to get it there, but it's the right thing to do. Why, you wonder? Well, pretend you are shaking someone's hand. Your right shoulder naturally falls forward. A name tag placed high on the right shoulder allows a person to look you in the eye and still read your name tag with his peripheral vision.

There is the notion that by placing your name tag over your heart you are communicating love and affection – nonsense. Putting it on the left just makes it more difficult for someone to read it.

"

A name tag is a cheat note posted on your chest for the benefit of others.

"

Other placement mistakes can cause uncomfortable moments. Ladies, a name tag is not a nipple guard. It's not appropriate to stick your name tag on or close to your breast. Those who are well-endowed should err on the side of caution and place a name tag even higher on the shoulder.

When conference planners opt to use name tags that hang around your neck, simply tie a knot in the lanyard to shorten the length of the string to make it easier for people to read. If left at full string length, these name tags are next to impossible to read without leaning down and gazing at a person's navel. Conference planners should provide shorter strings to solve this problem for their attendees.

At conferences, name tags hung on lanyards often double as carrying cases for hotel room keys, business cards, meal tickets and conference agendas. Don't cover your name with these items; instead put them in the holder behind the actual name tag so your name remains visible.

Name tags are not effective when they are stuck to ties, belts or purses. If you need to protect your jacket's fabric, consider a magnetic name tag.

A corporate name tag is okay providing the information is legible from a distance. Large, bold letters with high contrast between the background and lettering will maximize the benefits of a professionally-made name tag.

Here's a wise trick I learned from an associate. If, at the last minute, you are unable to attend a function, ask a colleague to remove your name tag from the reception table. By removing it, others registering won't see that you are a 'no-show'.

30 Remembering Names

Have you ever forgotten a name? Ever been caught off guard because you were supposed to introduce two acquaintances, but you've totally blanked? Of course you have – you're human. Forgetting names is a fact of life, yet for something that happens so routinely, it causes a lot of anxiety.

It's no wonder. To an individual, his name is very personal and hearing it spoken is like music to his ears. It can make a person feel important – or unimportant – when it's his name that's been remembered or forgotten. It can also make you feel like a real horse's you-know-what when you're the one who has forgotten someone's name.

Relax. Beating yourself up for being inept at remembering names is not going to make it any easier and it will likely perpetuate the problem. To alleviate pressure, the first thing to do is to accept that forgetting names happens, even for those who are usually good at remembering them.

In fact, I've noticed as my mind sifts through the thousands of names circling around in my head, that I'll second guess myself and play it safe by not using names at all until I am sure. This is probably a reaction from every now and again getting a name wrong when I thought I was right.

Not long ago a gentleman came over to me at a formal business function. I was certain he was a long lost contact I hadn't seen in a year. Unfortunately, he just looked like my long lost contact and was actually a partner in a firm I was hoping would contract my training services.

I not only called him by the wrong name, but I started a conversation with him to find out what he'd been doing the last year or so.

"

Forgetting names is a fact of life, yet for something that happens so routinely, it causes a lot of anxiety.

"

Mr. Partner was extremely gracious and didn't draw attention to my mistake. When another individual joined our conversation, even before I had a chance to introduce him incorrectly, he simply offered his hand and gave his proper name – what a classy guy.

I immediately admitted my mistake and apologized quietly while others in the group entered into conversation around us. Turns out, he was coming to tell me that he and his business partners had decided to hire me and they'd be in touch with me soon. Talk about putting my foot into my mouth, but what could I do after the fact? To lighten the situation I joked that I would teach his associates some name recalling techniques that actually work.

These bumps on the road of networking are bound to happen. Put them into perspective and understand that it's not the end of the world when they occur.

To learn how to remember names we must first understand why we forget them. Remembering names is difficult because we rarely pay attention during introductions.

The challenge exists because when you meet a new contact, your mind is too busy thinking about what you're going to say next, worrying about the impression you're making or daydreaming about items on your to-do list. With all of this mind-clutter, it's easy to miss the most important part of an introduction – learning the name of the person you are meeting.

So the first step to remembering names is to focus on the task at hand and actually listen carefully to the name when it's given to you.

As harsh as it may sound, it's easy to forget names because during the introduction, this new contact doesn't mean much in your life – yet.

Even if you listen to the name and hear it correctly, it's easy to forget because it has no context in your life. Without anchoring it to anything that is meaningful, your brain won't register the name as important information worth remembering.

> **The secret to remembering names is threefold: LISTEN, SOLIDIFY and THINK.**

If, however, you make a conscious effort to want to know who people are, you are more likely to remember names. Every time you meet someone, consider that person as your next client or next best friend. That will give your mind a reason to anchor the information.

Remembering names is a worthwhile skill to learn. It's amazing how impressed people are when you remember their names. What a compliment you are giving them.

When I wrote the column, it was my job to remember hundreds of people and their names. Comments were regularly made about my ability to remember people, not just their names, but information about them as well.

I found that the secret to remembering names is threefold:

Listen, Solidify and Think.

During the introduction I **listen**. Rather than worrying about what I'm going to say next or looking to see who else I can meet, I focus solely on the person I am meeting. Listening is much easier to do if you genuinely want to meet new people.

Next, I take a mental snapshot of the person to **solidify** the name and the image in my conscious mind (and probably in my subconscious mind, but I can't tell you that for sure because it's subconscious).

My mental snapshot includes a bit about the location where we're meeting and the person's name tag, which is why I'm a huge believer in the importance of name tags. They add a visual reminder of the name so I am sure to use it as well as the audio message. This image is the reason I can run into a person six months later and often pinpoint when and where we met. If we had a good chat or shared a laugh, I can usually remember a little about the person.

As they say, a picture is worth a thousand words. With a little practice and specific intent, solidifying freeze-framed mental pictures in your mind will give you something to recall when you see this person again. Hopefully, at the very least, this picture will be worth two words – the person's first and last names.

The most important strategy to remembering names is to **think**. After meeting people, I reflect on our conversations. What did we talk about? Who were they? What do they do? What did I like about them? How did we connect? Who introduced us? I don't spend hours obsessing over everyone I meet, but just a moment of conscious awareness after a conversation seems to pay dividends in the long run to winning the name game.

If I missed a name during an introduction, I look and listen for clues. In group discussions someone will usually reference a person's name, which is a great reminder. I read name tags and business cards. I ask mutual contacts, "Who is that again?" I read program books and event agendas to look for names of committee members, key volunteers and sponsors. I gather all the information I can and connect the dots.

> *Set mini-goals for yourself. For example, plan to remember two new contacts' names at the next event you attend. Consciously go through the three steps – Listen, Solidify and Think. After you leave, think about the people you've met and the next time you run into them, see how easy it is to recall their names.*

MY GOALS FOR REMEMBERING NAMES

_____

_____

_____

31 When Your Name has Been Forgotten

Is it possible? Could someone really have the nerve to forget your name? Let me ask you this. If you've forgotten names, isn't it safe to assume that others may forget your name?

Do not take offense when someone forgets your name. Memory recall isn't always the sharpest and people have a lot on their minds. It's arrogant to think that remembering your name is a top priority on a contact's to-do list, particularly when you've only met a few times.

It takes six to eight times of meeting someone casually before a person "gets" who you are and vice versa. Have you ever been sitting around a committee table and after several months of being on the same committee with someone, you look across the table and have that moment of clarity and say to yourself, "Oh yeah, hey, I know that person."?

Accept that others have distractions, problems and priorities in their lives. Do whatever you can to make it easy for people to know who you are, what you do and what you have to offer. The easier you make it for someone to remember your name, the more likely he is to remember it.

When saying hello to a casual contact, offer your first and last name again. This will eliminate the name-game pressure. Your effort to make others comfortable will encourage them to offer their name as well. A person who says, "Of course I know your name," could secretly be thrilled that you gave a kind reminder.

"

The easier you make it for someone to remember your name, the more likely he is to remember it.

"

If you find yourself in a group situation and your contact has not introduced you, he may have forgotten someone in the group's name (maybe yours). Simply extend your hand to others and introduce yourself to add comfort to a potentially uncomfortable moment.

To be extra considerate, add a one-line anecdote to explain your connection to the mutual contact. Your hint could ease the situation. For example, say, "Hi, I'm so and so. I just joined Bob's Rotary Club about a month ago." Immediately Bob will clue in to who you are and the conversation can flow from there.

Unfortunately, people will routinely give their first name only during introductions. Give your first and last name up front to make it easier for people to put you into context and introduce you to their contacts. Often it's the inclusion of the last name that will trigger an association that can lead to a conversation or discovery of a mutual friend.

32 When You Forget Someone's Name

When you're the person who has forgotten someone's name you may just need time for your memory to kick into gear, so continue the conversation and hope for a clue.

It's also acceptable to be honest, especially with someone you know you've only met once or twice. You could simply say, "I'm trying to remember where we first met" or "Forgive me, my brain's obviously not working up to snuff. What is your name again?" Be sure to listen when the name is repeated so you remember it for next time. Return the favour by offering your name, as well, to save others from having to ask.

If you've forgotten a name and you are required to introduce two people, simply ask, "Have you two met?" Naturally, the two will introduce themselves. That's when you listen to hear their names again.

33 Dining Etiquette

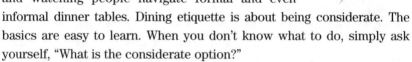

Dining etiquette is a lost art form. Nothing reminds me of this more than sitting at a business function and watching people navigate formal and even informal dinner tables. Dining etiquette is about being considerate. The basics are easy to learn. When you don't know what to do, simply ask yourself, "What is the considerate option?"

For example, it's inconsiderate to chew with your mouth open or to talk with food in your mouth. It's inconsiderate to lick your fingers, especially when you are about to shake someone's hand. It's inconsiderate to shovel food into your mouth or to focus so much on food that you ignore others at the table. It's inconsiderate to put your dirty napkin on the table for others to see while they are still eating. It's inconsiderate to monopolize the conversation. You get the picture.

PLACE SETTINGS

Solids are on the left, liquids on the right. That means your bread plate is on the left side beside your forks, and your drinking glasses are on the right side above the knife and spoons. To make it easy to remember, make the "OK" sign with your fingers with both hands. You'll notice your left hand forms a 'b' (for bread) and your right forms a 'd' shape (for drinks). As the first person to sit at the table, this trick will help you start the plates and glasses correctly.

If the table settings have been started incorrectly and you are forced to use the wrong bread plate and drink glasses, be considerate by not drawing attention to the situation. This could embarrass the person who started using the settings incorrectly.

You can, however, simply move the available bread plate to the proper side and once you've taken a sip from your glass, you can place it on the right side – which happens to be on the right side.

NAPKINS

Once seated, immediately place your napkin on your lap. Do not tuck it into your shirt to use it as a bib. To avoid splashing on your clothes, eat carefully and at a comfortable pace.

When you place the napkin on your lap, fold the furthest few inches of the napkin over on itself. This way, you can use that inside edge of the napkin to dab your mouth. When you place it back on your lap, fold the soiled end back over on itself so you will protect your clothing and hide the mess.

Please do not lick your fingers; that's why you have a napkin. Never use your napkin as a tissue to blow your nose.

If you need to leave during the meal, say a soft "Excuse me" to those on either side of you and then leave your napkin on your chair, not on the table. When you leave at the end of the meal, you can put your napkin on the table to let the server know you are not returning.

USING SILVERWARE IN NORTH AMERICA

Choose silverware from the outside first and work your way in towards the plate. Utensils placed horizontally across the top of your place setting are for coffee and dessert. Technically, you should have new silverware for each course. If the server insists you keep your silverware, place it on your bread plate, not on the tablecloth, because it's inconsiderate to soil the tablecloth with your utensils. Do not point or gesture with your silverware. Never lick your knife.

Cut one piece of food at a time: we are not children. Although it is acceptable to use the Continental eating style that would be considered appropriate and elegant in European culture, the North American eating style is recommended while on this continent. As they say, "When in Rome...."

AMERICAN STYLE

When cutting food, the fork should be held in your left hand and the knife in your right. To take a bite of food, lay your knife on the top-right edge of your plate and transfer your fork to your right hand. Bring the food to your mouth with fork tines facing upward.

CONTINENTAL STYLE

This practice is considered more formal and is customary in other parts of the world. Rather than changing hands to cut and eat, the fork and knife remain in the same hand throughout the meal. The knife is in your right hand and your fork is kept in your left, positioned with tines facing down.

GENERAL MANNERS

Keep the pace of your tablemates as you eat.

The meal officially begins when the host takes the first bite. Wait for all guests to be seated and served before you begin to eat.

Do not talk while someone is speaking from the microphone; it is inconsiderate and can make it difficult for a speaker to concentrate. Regardless of how quiet you think you are whispering, you'll never be quiet enough to avoid irritating those around you who are trying to listen.

Don't go to an event hungry. It will make it easier for you to focus on the people rather than the food. Buffets at business functions are not the same as "all-you-can-eat free-for-alls" at restaurants. Take your fair share, but not so much that you look like an "oinker".

Elbows should not be placed on the table until the dinner plates have been taken.

Eat quietly. Avoid smacking sounds or hitting your teeth with your silverware. The irritation of sharing a meal with a person who constantly grinds his fork to his teeth is equivalent to hearing fingernails scratching on a chalkboard.

When eating hors d'oeuvres, stand close to a table so you can rest your glass and eat comfortably. When plates are not available, only take one or two hors d'oeuvres at a time.

Use the water glass when toasting the Queen. Do not clink glasses during a toast. Raise your glass, make eye contact with your tablemates, and nod your head slightly. After the toast is complete, take a sip of the liquid to complete the ritual.

Make sure that all the words you say at a dinner table or in a buffet line are appropriate. Health issues, bodily functions, accidents, etc. are not welcomed subjects for mealtime.

CIRCULATING ITEMS

It is your responsibility to notice and begin to circulate items directly in front of you. Pass items to the right; however, offer the bread to your left, then choose your own piece from the basket before passing it to the right. Pass salt and pepper as a set, even if only one is requested.

BREAD AND BUTTER

The bread plate is on your left side. Using the knife provided with the butter or your personal butter knife provided on your bread plate, scoop butter directly from the dish to your bread plate – not directly to your bread. Break a piece of bread, butter it (one piece at a time) and eat it.

Eat everything that goes towards your mouth in one bite. Food that goes up to your mouth does not go back down to your plate. Watching a person make a butter sandwich and proceed to gnaw off a hunk of bread and put the rest down is not enjoyable, albeit a frequent occurrence.

EATING SOUP

Draw the spoon away from you to fill it with soup. Quietly sip the soup from the side of the spoon. Tilt the bowl away from you to get the last drops. Do not sip directly from the bowl.

To eliminate soup drips falling from the bottom of your spoon, simply dip the under edge of your spoon into the top of the soup rather than wiping it on the edge of your bowl. Yes, remarkably, this works. When finished eating the soup, rest the spoon on the plate, below the bowl. If there is no plate, you can leave the spoon in the bowl.

SALAD

The chef should prepare salad in bite-sized pieces. However, if the pieces of salad are too large to eat, use the edge of your salad fork to cut them into smaller pieces. As a last resort, use your dinner knife to cut the lettuce, but that means you will need a new knife for your main course. If you have to keep your soiled knife, set it on your bread plate.

CONCLUSION OF MEAL

In North America, place utensils at the 4:20 position to signal that you are finished your meal. The fork tines face up and the knife blade should face the fork. This will protect the server from accidentally being cut should the knife slide. Again, it's about being considerate.

It is rude to stack your plates, push them away or hand them to the server at formal dinners. Place your loosely folded napkin, soiled side down and hidden, on the table just as you stand to leave, not before.

34 Objectives for Attending Events

The main reason you go to business functions is to meet people and reconnect with contacts – not to talk with your colleagues and friends. Save those personal conversations for personal time.

Events are not the time to sell your product or pitch your latest idea nor are they where the bulk of your relationships will be made. Group settings are for introductions, small chat and light business talk. They are a great place to identify connections so you can follow up outside of the event – which is where the strong business relationships are built.

When I say "event or function" I mean anything that is a formalized activity with potential for interaction with people. Some examples are a charity gala, a speaker's series, a lunch and learn, or a breakfast club.

The best part about business events is that they collect people with a common denominator for you. Depending on the function, the common denominator will change, but basically, others are there to meet new people and reconnect with current contacts too. Your job is to show up and connect with them. If you don't, chances are your competition will.

> **"**
>
> **Group settings are for introductions, small chat and light business talk.**
>
> **"**

Some events are more effective for networking than others as we'll explore in Section 4, but as a general rule, if you show up consistently and persistently and you present a welcoming, genuine professional image, you can't help but build a network.

35 Making Events Worthwhile

Have you ever calculated what it truly costs you to attend an event?

As a rough estimate, take your hourly rate (which may be different than your hourly wage) and multiply it by the number of hours needed for the event. Add the ticket price, any extra costs such as drink tickets and auction prizes, expenses incurred getting to the function and the investment needed to dress for the event and you have calculated a base amount needed for your attendance. Don't forget to consider the intangible costs inherent in being away from your office or your family.

As you can imagine, each event can get pricey. Don't get me wrong; this math exercise is not to give you an excuse to avoid networking events, but rather, it's a wake up call so that when you do go to events you are mindful to make them worthwhile.

The reality is, if you want to build the ultimate network, then you have to go where there are people. The potentially high cost associated with networking is the exact reason why you must make good business decisions when it comes to attending or sending employees to events.

It's simply impossible to calculate the true return on your time invested when networking. In my case, I owe my entire career to the chain of events that started with a single Saturday morning reception.

What price tag would you put on meeting your biggest client, finding your best friend or landing your dream job? There may be tangible financial benefits that can make such connections measurable but the quality of life and the intangibles that come from having the ultimate network are priceless.

It's equally impossible to put a figure on what it costs you to NOT network. How can you calculate what you don't know could happen? Had I chosen to stay in bed that Saturday morning, my life's path would arguably be quite different. Sure, I would have eventually found success, but I doubt my path would have been the same or that I would have accomplished so much in so little time.

What is the opportunity cost for continuing to struggle to meet new people or reach your sales targets? The time spent cold calling and advertising to attract new clients could be better spent building your network and setting the foundation for long-term success.

Networking naysayers show up once or twice, don't meet any new clients and make a judgement call that all networking events are a waste of time based on inefficient efforts. They don't give the natural processes of networking and relationship building the chance they deserve.

Events, when used properly, can be a gold mine for your business networking efforts, yet so few professionals really grasp the opportunities to their fullest.

It boggles my mind how companies will spend $1500 to buy a table at a business or charity event and allow their executives, sales reps and staff to sit together and spend all night talking. They spend all this money so their employees can move their water cooler conversation of the day to a very expensive round table at night. What a waste of company resources.

Consider the impact had those same employees spent the night talking with current and potential clients and reconnecting with contacts. At the very least, cut the number from the company in half and invite guests to join the table instead. Then, half of the faces in the group are potential business opportunities for the company.

Variations of this ineffective approach to attending events happen all the time.

If you've ever left an event and thought to yourself, "Okay, there are five hours of my life I will never get back," then you're not alone. Unless you are a natural born schmoozer, business functions can be intimidating and difficult to navigate to make them worthwhile.

The good news is that you can make attending events valuable. They are just one part of the networking process but they can be catalysts for your success as they were for mine. It just takes some *perspective*, *preparation* and *practice*. Tackle one idea at a time and build momentum until networking becomes second nature.

Natural born networkers should stick with what's already working for them. Incorporate your personality with the mechanics of working your way through a crowd. Use the tips that follow to tweak your talents and to ensure you maximize opportunities to achieve success.

36 Including Spouses and Friends

Your decision to proactively build your business network means some of your habits will have to change. Talking all night with your best friend at business functions or treating business functions as dates with your spouse will not garner the results you want.

Share your goals with your family, friends and work colleagues. Ask them to support you in your business-networking efforts. A buddy system can be great as long as you're on the same page. Choosing to build your network together requires you to detach from one another's hip when at public functions. "Birds of a feather flock together", so be sure your networking buddy is up to speed on business etiquette and is projecting a professional image as well. Ask your friend for feedback on how you present yourself and vice-versa.

> **Business functions are not the time to highlight and solve your spouse's inadequacies.**

Spouses may need to shift their attitudes and expectations to support you as you build your ultimate network. Spouses should complement your efforts – not cause you undue stress at business functions. This is why it is especially important to share your goals and expectations with your family.

Be sure your significant other understands what you're trying to accomplish, that it won't happen overnight and that the commitment required to be successful will be intense. To minimize last minute stress, it's helpful to keep your spouse in the loop and schedule events in advance.

When you attend an event on behalf of your company, you are on your company's time. Your spouse should be aware of your work expectations in advance and should allow you the freedom to mingle in a professional manner. Remember, business functions are not dates.

When you sit at a dinner table, don't sit next to your spouse or friend. You can be more effective sitting across from each other, leaving the chairs beside you for new contacts and other acquaintances. That will leave you plenty to talk about on the way home – or on a real date night.

If you do take your spouse, remember to treat each other with respect. Business functions are not the time to highlight and solve your spouse's inadequacies.

Recently, I sat beside a couple at a black tie gala event. Obviously, the black tie environment was not the husband's forté and the wife wouldn't let him forget it. Every time he opened his mouth to speak, she gave him the evil eye and the nudge, that we could all feel, under the table.

By trying to keep him in line, she drew attention to his shortcomings and turned what could have been a fun night into an uncomfortable situation for everyone at the table.

If your spouse lacks business savvy and dining etiquette, work with him or her outside of the function in a constructive way, but when you're in public, just let it go. Drawing attention to your spouse's deficiencies will just help others see them.

It's a rare couple who can complement each other's networking efforts. I'm privileged to know several and it's easy to see the difference between those who move in business circles well as a couple and those who don't.

If your spouse isn't into it, doesn't "get it" or you feel s/he cramps your style, it's best (and easier) to leave him/her at home, attend your function solo and then spend quality time with your partner afterwards.

37 Before An Event

Would you walk into a meeting with a client unprepared? Of course not. You would risk looking unorganized while wasting time for both of you. Preparing for a business function should be given the same respect.

Regardless of the time of day or how you choose to fill your hours, the value of your time remains constant. An hour spent in a boardroom "costs" you the same amount as an hour spent at a function. Why wouldn't you give the same consideration to business functions as you do to time spent in company meetings? When you network, you are engaging in an equally important business activity.

This doesn't mean that for every function you'll have to write a full report, create an agenda, consider objectives and analyze anticipated outcomes. However, you should at least formulate some thoughts as to the purpose of the event and have a game plan of what you're going to do when you're there.

Before you go to a function, determine your intention for attending the event and do your pre-event homework. Visit the organization's website. Who is on the board? Who is sponsoring the event? Is anyone being honoured? Who will likely attend? Who is the host? Why are you going? How does this event fit with your focus board? (Refer to Chapter 4 on The Strategy.) What is the dress code? Who do you hope to meet? What is the purpose of the event?

Check the agenda. When is the best time to arrive? When your time is limited, the priority for your attendance should be the informal portion of any event. That's when guests mingle and you can connect with the greatest number of people. Arriving just in time to hear the speaker or to sit for dinner doesn't allow you much opportunity to network.

Most people leave immediately at the conclusion of the formal portion of an event so it's best to go early before the main event or meal in order to catch people you hope to meet. If your schedule permits, plan to spend extra time after the event to engage in conversation with stragglers. This is excellent relationship-building time because there are relatively few people left in the room.

If you have a purpose and good understanding as to why you are going to an event, it will help you to know when you can leave. You don't always have to stay for the entire event. If you have objectives and you fill them early, you can adjust your departure time accordingly.

This sort of targeted approach for maximizing your attendance at events is handy when your to-do list is overloaded and you want to go home to your family. Don't make a big deal about sneaking out early; just do what you came to do and quietly excuse yourself.

Before you enter an event, take a mental note of your attitude and self confidence level. If your mood is projecting anything less than a warm, welcoming, professional image, then have a talk with yourself, adjust your mood and get your act together. Find your smile before you see someone else's face at the event.

There are days when you may not feel like going to another event or speaking with another person. That's natural. I'll admit to having those days. But, if you're committed to building your network, you can't sit at home watching television and eating popcorn, hoping people will "get" who you are. Ironically, it's usually the events that you attend when you don't feel like it that prove to be the best times.

A good way to shift your attitude is to focus on others. Helping and connecting other people always bring a warm fuzzy feeling to the potentially harsh reality of business. By focusing on others you can forget about the crummy experiences that happened earlier in your day and enjoy the company of the people in the room.

If you're not feeling confident, review your personal adjective list created in the Business of YOU section. Focus on the bigger picture and your long-term objectives. Envision life with the ultimate network.

Before each event, regardless of your mood, review the definition of business networking and set realistic expectations. Be aware of your own agenda, then forget it. Yes, you want to connect with the people you came to meet, but it's a balancing act between accomplishing your goals and taking your eyes off yourself so you can genuinely connect with others. Have purpose, but don't be calculating.

Remind yourself that it is your responsibility to make it easy for people to know who you are, what you do and what you have to offer.

Take care of the Business of YOU before you go. Are you dressed and groomed in a professional manner? Are your clothes clean and pressed? Do they match the dress code? Dealing with the Business of YOU first will give you the confidence to stop worrying about the impression you're going to make.

Review the event notice. What do you need to take with you? For instance, do you need a cheque book, ticket, parking pass or directions to the location?

Such a routine may seem tedious, but after a few times, running over this checklist will become automatic. Once you're all set and ready for your event, put a smile on your face, grab a stack of business cards and get on your way.

PRE-EVENT CHECKLIST

Details:

✓ Ticket
✓ Location/directions
✓ Parking pass
✓ Dress code

The Business of YOU

✓ Dressed professionally and appropriately
✓ Well-groomed
✓ Attitude adjusted
✓ Genuinely interested in connecting with others
✓ Feeling confident (review Top 20 Confidence List from Chapter 24)
✓ Smile on face

The Fundamentals

✓ Business cards: inbox/outbox (purse cleaned, if applicable)
✓ Handshake: ready for firm, web-to-web grip with solid wrist
✓ Name tag: first and last name and company name, high on right shoulder
✓ Dining etiquette: reminded to be considerate of others

The Strategy

✓ Reviewed meaning and objectives for proper business networking
✓ Checked agenda – determined best time to go and scheduled enough time
✓ Determined purpose for attending
✓ Reviewed list of sponsors/committee members

38 Arrival

Set your intention and check your attitude as you arrive at the function. The last time you should worry about "YOU" is when you enter the room. Forget your agenda, stop worrying about your overloaded to-do list, clear your mind of self-doubt and get ready to enjoy the process.

How you behave at public events will set the foundation for your personal brand and reputation. The event begins when you arrive in the parking lot and ends when you drive away. Parking lots are excellent places to meet new people who are attending the same event. If you are concerned you won't know many people, it's a non-intimidating place to practise starting conversations with new contacts.

"

The last time you should worry about "YOU" is when you enter the room.

"

Keep focused on the other people at the event. They will appreciate your genuine interest in them and your selfless nature will be noticed, even if it is subtle.

To build event-going confidence, find your own routine. When you enter, pause for a moment to scan the room. Who's there? What's happening? What's the tone of the room? Where are the amenities? Who do you know? Who do you want to know?

Take care of housekeeping duties first. Register, pay your admission, affix your name tag, check table seating and buy drink tickets. Then you are free to mingle. If you're not a fan of conversations with strangers, use the registration process to practise engaging in dialogue with new contacts. This warm-up will help you prepare to connect with known and unknown people as you circulate through the room.

Work your way to and from a determined point in the room. It will establish a sense of direction for you and encourage you to meet more people because you know you have to complete your "figure 8" or get to the bar and back before dinner is called.

> **"**
>
> **How you behave at public events will set the foundation for your personal brand and reputation.**
>
> **"**

After you've entered and taken a moment to scan the room, then make your first move. Yes, walking into a room full of strangers can be intimidating. Relax. One day the situation will reverse itself. You'll know everyone in the room and you'll be greeting newcomers to make them feel comfortable.

No need to worry if you find yourself left alone for a few minutes in between conversations or before you find your first conversation partner. Instinctively we don't want to look like the loner in the room so we beeline to the one person we know best and settle into the comfort zone for the night. By taking a breath and slowing down the entry process you may see someone else or allow time for a new contact to be made.

Rest assured, people will not point and laugh at you and think you are an unpopular loser with whom no one wants to talk. I haven't seen it happen yet. However, I have seen the look of panic on the faces of those who are left alone. It must be residual psychological effects from school playgrounds because I've not met anyone who is completely comfortable standing on his own in a room full of people.

Time on your own will give you a chance to regroup and determine where you want to go next, allowing you to take a proactive approach to mingling. It will also give others a chance to approach you. Granted, if you do remain on your own for too long – like, say, for most of the event – you will look awkward and out of place.

It's easier to meet people at the beginning of an event. People are still warming up and getting into "networking mode." Chances are their friends have not arrived yet and event hosts will be waiting for people to fill the room. It's much less intimidating to walk into a room occupied by just a few people than to walk into a room filled with an active crowd where everyone is already engaged in conversation.

39 Mingling Formula™

Have you ever wondered how some people float through a room seemingly effortlessly? They appear to connect with people in a matter of seconds and then move to the next person without hesitation. It helps to know many people, but guaranteed, there was a time when that social butterfly didn't know anyone in the room.

Rarely do I go to an event now where I don't know a good majority of the attendees, but that wasn't always the case. Eight years ago, I wouldn't have known which room to walk into, let alone who was there. At some point, a room full of strangers became a room full of contacts. Mingling made that happen.

As my company developed, I learned that mingling was a real barrier for people so I took a closer look at how one mingles effectively and voilà – my Mingling Formula was developed:

1 Initiate dialogue

2 Create a mini-bond

3 Get and/or give contact information (or at least know how to get it)

4 Move on

5 Repeat often

It's that simple. Once you've tackled each element, you'll be ready and able to make your way through any crowd effortlessly. Anyone who knows more than two people (his parents) has successfully completed the Mingling Formula thousands of times in life. Even if you don't formalize it, the Mingling Formula is how all relationships begin.

Think about it. You meet. You start talking. You decide you like each other so you exchange contact information. Then you leave. You already practise this process daily. Maybe not all elements of the Mingling Formula occur during each encounter, but variations of the formula happen routinely.

Have confidence that life has already prepared you to be a master at mingling. What you've lived every day of your life is the same process that will help you maximize business functions.

Step one, initiating dialogue, happens frequently. It could be as simple as talking with the cashier when you buy something at the store or commenting on the weather when you share an elevator. Initiating dialogue does not mean you have to have a full-blown conversation.

Mingling at an event may seem more intimidating because it's a formalized environment and there are more people with whom you can engage in the process. A crowd is no more than a bunch of individuals gathered in the same place. The fact that you are among the crowd means you already have something in common with others who are there.

As we discussed earlier, the keys to effective business networking and building confidence come from *perspective*, *preparation* and *practice*. The same rules apply when engaging with new contacts and becoming a master-mingler.

PERSPECTIVE

Understand that others go to events to connect with people just as you do and many of them have the same fears and hesitations when it comes to talking with strangers.

PREPARATION

Know the Mingling Formula. Have potential topics ready to discuss and your favourite conversation starters ready to go.

PRACTICE

The more you experience the Mingling Formula the easier it will become. One day, engaging in conversation with strangers at functions will be as comfortable as talking with your closest associates.

40 Initiating Dialogue

The logical beginning of every relationship is conversation. Initiating dialogue is an important first step; without the onset of a conversation, how will you get to know someone?

When we were young, our parents taught us to not talk to strangers. For many, this remains imbedded in their attitudes as they set out to build a network. To build your ultimate network, you're going to have to let this philosophy go and start talking with people you don't know yet.

The best way to initiate dialogue is to simply make eye contact and say, "Hello." Rarely will people turn away from you provided you present a professional, confident and inviting image. If you are, and they still snub you, that's their problem, not yours. When you use this approach, prepare to lead the conversation somewhere. It's uncomfortable to stop a conversation after hello.

> **"**
>
> **The best way to initiate dialogue is to simply make eye contact and say, "Hello."**
>
> **"**

When looking for a conversation partner in a crowded room there are three likely scenarios that make it easy to initiate dialogue:

1 fun, inviting groups

2 white-knuckled loners who look uncomfortable and will welcome your attempt to initiate dialogue

3 familiar faces

When it comes to initiating dialogue, accept that for the most part, conversation openers will not be that original or exciting. It's the formality of the beginning of any relationship. True connections develop thanks to the direction of the dialogue after it's been instigated.

Use your surroundings to strike up a conversation. Situational dialogue offers common ground and can lead to laughs and further conversation. Take notice of what's happening around you as this is natural ammunition for great conversations.

It helps to have some key questions and conversation starters ready to use in those potentially uncomfortable first few moments after an introduction. Having several opening lines and topics on the tip of your tongue will give you confidence and clear your head when being introduced to new contacts. This should make it easier to listen and subsequently to remember a person's name.

As a note of caution, preparation is important, but it's equally important to be natural and act in the moment. If you sound like a robot and ask the same question every time you meet someone new or ask questions that don't have a natural flow that fits the environment, you run the risk of sounding contrived and phoney. Having a variety of starters is helpful to make initiating dialogue easier over time.

Here are some suggested open-ended questions that can get, and keep, conversations flowing:

- How do the two of you know each other?
- What's your connection to this event?
- What keeps you busy when you're not at functions like this?
- How are you involved with this organization?
- How did you find out about tonight?
- Are you working on any interesting projects?

The answers to these questions will lead into more in-depth dialogue. Avoid using anything that is too farfetched. I've heard some ask questions like: "If you were a fruit, what fruit would you be?" or "Where's the one place in the world you'd prefer to be?"

Sure, the answers may be revealing, but it's tough to be taken seriously as a business person when asking abstract questions. Some appreciate originality, but this type of probing will stretch people out of their comfort zones before a mini-bond has been established. For the record, I've only heard the fruit question popped once – but it has stuck in my memory ever since.

Uncomfortable silence often occurs when two people are introduced by a third party and neither offers any conversational tidbit to get the ball rolling after the handshakes. It goes something like this: "Nice to meet you." "Yes, nice to meet you too." Then both look back to the introducer for a prolonged session of dead air.

More than once, I've introduced two people and after the handshakes, one of the contacts just walks away. I have one associate who does this frequently. When I asked about the reason behind the "meet and run" pattern, the response was, "I don't want to interrupt or impose". This is likely the reason many people don't stick around to engage in conversation after casual introductions.

I recall one particularly uncomfortable situation when a contact entered a conversation to talk with me. After I introduced her to the person I had been talking with, she shook her hand and then vanished! We were both left feeling bewildered. To my original conversation partner, her abrupt exit was insulting.

For me, I was annoyed and confused as to why my contact interrupted a conversation already in progress and then purposely or accidentally insulted my associate because she had no intention of continuing the communication with us.

The "talk to the hand" or "I'm too good to talk to you" impression that is given in this type of situation is uncomfortable and insulting to the person being snubbed – even if it's unintentional.

Initiating dialogue is much easier when you project an image that communicates that you want to talk with someone. The more signals you can send that say, "I'm approachable and yes, I would like to talk with you too," the more others will feel comfortable conversing with you.

MY FIVE FAVOURITE CONVERSATION STARTERS

1 _____

2 _____

3 _____

4 _____

5 _____

41 Small But Meaningful Chat

> **"**
>
> **The goal of conversation at functions is to determine a reason and desire to connect outside of the event.**
>
> **"**

A successful conversation is much like a tennis game – back and forth with each participant equally enthused. Once the dialogue has begun, the conversation should flow from there.

Mastering small talk will help you find common ground to create a mini-bond with new contacts. Small talk may feel trite and unimportant, but it's the small talk that leads to the big talk outside of the event.

The goal of conversation at functions is to establish enough common ground to determine a reason to connect outside of the event.

It's not to become best friends on the spot. Although it's nice when those instant connections happen, mostly that's not the case.

Ultimately, the decision each person has to make during this initial contact is whether or not there is enough connection to warrant future interaction. It's during these small conversations at events that the "I like you, trust you, and think you are competent" opinions mentioned throughout this book start to form.

Actual business talk is quite limited at functions. Learning what people do and perhaps about some of their big developments or projects is about the extent of the business talk expected. Deeper connections are formed through finding common ground that is not work-related.

There is a balance between too much and too little business talk. If you don't talk business at all you may miss an opportunity to communicate who you are, what you do and what you have to offer and that you are competent in your field.

> **"**
> **Match the depth of dialogue to the environment.**
> **"**

However, if you talk about your work too much you run the risk of boring others. Too much "shop talk" can easily put a damper on an evening. Watch for cues from your conversation partners. How are they responding to the conversation with you? Are they engaged? Are they obviously looking for a new conversation partner? Are they listening to and understanding what you are saying? Are you giving them more information than they expect, want or need? Are you monopolizing the conversation and not allowing others a chance to share ideas or ask questions?

Match the depth of dialogue to the environment. You don't want to let people overhear confidential or inappropriate information. Plus, talk that is too deep at business functions can lead to heated conversations. New contacts could be put on edge. Over-heated conversations can quickly be subdued by simply making a closing agreeable statement that offers little room for a rhetorical comment. This tactic will diffuse the situation quickly and without incident.

For example, say with a smile, "Well that's one issue we're not going to solve tonight" or simply close the conversation with, "I certainly understand your perspective," minus the "but" that is sitting on the tip of your tongue.

> **"**
> **You will win points for social graces if you are the bigger person and cool potentially fiery situations.**
> **"**

You won't win points for always having to be "right." You may win the debate while making someone else look bad, but in the end, you'll make yourself look worse. You will, however, win points for social graces if you are the bigger person and cool potentially fiery situations.

You have to know when to let go and kill the discussion even if you believe you are correct on the issue. In the grand scheme of things, we must value the opinions of others and accept that it is not important to win every debate. The last thing you want to do is to appear as a know-it-all who must end conversations as the perceived winner.

Debates definitely have a place in conversation and can be a great way to help you get to know people, but pick the time and place and be aware of the company around you. Intense debates can lead to arguments that rarely provide a comfortable environment at business and social functions, especially for those who aren't interested in the topic at hand.

Obviously, discussions around usually taboo subjects such as religion and politics will be discussed and debated at religious or political events. Even then, you want to be sure that the intensity level is kept to a professional standard. Earning a reputation as a hothead doesn't make it easy for people to like you, trust you or think you're competent.

Keep a close watch on the body language of others. Likely, as the conversation intensifies, you'll notice onlookers become proportionately more tense. That's a good cue to cool it.

Another confrontational conversation style is playing "top it." Although at first everyone seems to be enjoying the banter, each turn becomes an exercise to see who can say something bigger, better and more profound to outshine the other.

This habit can stem from a lack of self-confidence and a need to flex one's muscles to sound credible, but it backfires. "Top it" conversationalists come across as arrogant. They make the other person feel uncomfortable and unworthy. One-upmanship is a definite no-no.

Let others have the glory every now and again. A person may be sharing what he perceives to be an exciting story about a recent trip; let him tell it and bask in the moment. There's nothing worse than having someone pipe in to say, "Yeah, been there ten times; no biggie, there are better places to go."

You'll squash the person's excitement and you'll purposely make another person feel substandard. No one cares that you've been to the destination ten times if the information is offered with a condescending tone. However, input that is supportive and non-judgemental is always welcomed.

When it comes to small talk, don't think that you must say something strikingly intelligent each time you speak. Your words may be forgotten, but how you make people feel will be remembered.

No doubt small talk can get a little dull after a while. So, take it upon yourself to make it interesting. To prepare for conversations, choose your five favourite safe topics. These will make it easy for you to swing an otherwise stale conversation into one that makes you a genuinely enthusiastic conversationalist.

> **"**
> **Your words may be forgotten, but how you make people feel will be remembered.**
> **"**

Have you ever been in a conversation that just wasn't clicking, then all of a sudden the mood changes and you both have a smile on your face as the conversation starts firing on all cylinders? That's because you found common ground. It occurs when two people have an interest in the same topic.

> **"**
>
> **By determining in advance what interests you, half of the equation for stimulating conversation is complete.**
>
> **"**

By determining in advance what interests you, half of the equation for stimulating conversation is complete. Now, your job is to guide the conversation from topic to topic until you solve the other important half of the equation – what's of interest to your new contact.

For example, one of my favourite topics is travel. Whenever conversation is directed to stories of where people have been, where they are going next, or where they would like to travel, I'm automatically enthused and interested.

On the flip side, there are topics that will start and my eyes will glaze over and my mind will start to wander. These uninteresting topics for me may be someone else's hot topics. The idea is to find the topics you both enjoy. If you find your conversation partner disengaging, then change the subject.

Your arsenal of prepared conversation topics will give you ammunition when a conversation hits a lull and you need to give it some energy.

MY FIVE FAVOURITE CONVERSATION TOPICS

1 _____

2 _____

3 _____

4 _____

5 _____

What information do you need to know about a person to categorize your contact? (Refer to Chapter 53 on Categorizing Contacts) Are there relevant details, in addition to your prepared favourite topics, that can help you decide if this person is in fact a qualified prospect in your target market without specifically discussing business?

For example, if you own a wellness store, it would be helpful to direct the conversation to learn if the contact takes special care of his health, spends time exercising outdoors or frequents the gym.

DETAILS TO KNOW ABOUT OTHERS
THAT WILL HELP ME CATEGORIZE CONTACTS

_____

_____

_____

_____

_____

_____

_____

The real key to great conversations is to relax. Let the conversation flow naturally. That's easiest to do when you're fully engaged and genuinely interested in the conversation topic and the person with whom you are talking.

42 Listening

Your most important responsibility during a conversation is to listen. For some people, it's also the most difficult part of the conversation process. Listening requires focus, genuine interest and a desire to want to hear and process what another is saying. It also requires you to stop talking.

As you develop your conversation skills, make a conscious effort to become an excellent listener. The best advantage is that you will be a pleasant addition to any conversation. Good listeners are always welcomed – and needed.

Without someone to listen, people would just walk around talking to themselves. There are a few who don't like to share the airwaves and I bet they would just talk to themselves if it were socially acceptable, but it's not.

When you listen closely and purposely, you learn powerful information that is otherwise missed.

Most people like to hear themselves talk, so finding someone who will listen is quite refreshing. Pretending to listen won't separate you from your competition, but actually hearing and processing what a person has to say and then responding to it appropriately will.

A client once told me she was not a good listener. When I asked her why, she said she's usually not interested in what the other person is saying. It was a brutally honest and refreshing comment that reflects the reality of human nature. We only care about what we care about and we tend to shut out the rest.

Having your five favourite safe topics should help you manoeuver a conversation to ensure the subject matter appeals to your interests. It's easier to listen when you want to hear the information being communicated.

However, effective listening won't just happen by finding topics that interest you. The second important part of the solution is to have a genuine interest in the person who is doing the talking. Accomplishing this may require an attitude adjustment on your part. Perhaps focusing on your greater goal of building your ultimate network will help you find the motivation to take a genuine interest in other people and what they are saying.

The sooner you can accept the importance of listening, the sooner you can perfect the skill and start connecting with your ultimate network.

Listening well takes patience. It means not saying everything your brain thinks it wants you to say. It's rude to interrupt people as they speak.

Show you are listening by fully engaging with your conversation partner. Maintain eye contact (every seven or eight seconds glance away to avoid a hypnotic trance), nod your head, ask relevant questions and make statements that have relevance to the topic being discussed.

> **Part of the solution is to have a genuine interest in the person who is doing the talking.**

Be aware of your body language. What are you saying without speaking? Wandering eyes and a disengaged stance will give the impression you are not interested. This type of body language will send the message that you want to talk with someone else, rather than projecting a genuine, welcoming professional image that will encourage people to like you, trust you and think you are competent.

When you are fortunate to find a good listener, don't take advantage of the situation by doing all the talking. It's difficult for a person to listen for an extended length of time. Monopolizing the conversation to tell someone all about you restricts the back and forth dialogue required for the two of you to develop a mutually beneficial relationship. Keep an eye on your listener's body language and ask yourself, if you were that person, would you still be interested in listening to you?

43 Creating Mini-Bonds

The second step in the Mingling Formula is essential to change casual contacts into business relationships. Learning how to create mini-bonds, or establish rapport with new contacts, will make you a master at building genuine business relationships.

Without this, there is no reason to move to Step 3, which is getting and giving contact information. Rushing through the mini-bond step leads to mere business card collecting and ineffective networking.

The key to creating a mini-bond is actually caring about the other person. You can't fake this. It's tough to hide a genuine dislike for people and displaying a negative, uninterested attitude won't help people like you, trust you or think you are competent.

If you truly don't like people, you may want to reconsider your decision to be in the people business. Overcoming a disinterest in others will require a shift in thinking. Do all you can to appreciate the talents and personalities of people you meet. Finding the best in others while taking the focus off yourself is a good place to start.

> **The more respect you show to others, the more respect you will earn for yourself.**

What characteristics do people you connect with possess? What do you enjoy most about people? What is the difference between people you like and those you like less? Is it common interest, mutual friends or similar humour?

Years ago a friend told me, "Love is not what you feel about another person; it's how another person makes you feel about yourself." I don't know if it's a famous quote or where it came from, but it has stuck with me.

As you build your network, you will notice that the better you make others feel about themselves, the more people will be attracted to you. Setting others at ease will make them feel comfortable and they will want to be around you. Conversely, if you are harsh, abrupt and uninterested, it will have the opposite effect. The more respect you show to others, the more respect you will earn for yourself.

Body language can make a huge impact on your ability to establish rapport. Are your actions sending the right message? Do you seem engaged in the conversation? Are your eyes wandering to find someone more interesting? Are you "present" or are you worrying about your dry cleaning?

Make solid eye contact and square your body to your conversation partner. Focusing solely on the person will make him feel important. Surprisingly, 30 seconds of engaged dialogue has more impact than 10 minutes spent in disengaged, phoney conversation.

Sharing a laugh or inside joke goes a long way to establishing a sense of ease and camaraderie.

Once you identify your favourite topics it will be easier to find connections with people. This will enable you to steer conversations in directions that interest you, thereby maximizing your chance to create a mini-bond based on common interest.

As you get to know contacts better, you will find the conversation with them will become more personal, more fluent and more comfortable. This level of comfort is imperative to take casual contacts to the next level, providing you don't cross any inappropriate lines and personal boundaries.

"

There's a natural back and forth that goes with the release of information that allows a relationship to develop to a deeper connection.

"

There's a natural back and forth that goes with the release of information that allows a relationship to develop to a deeper connection. A block in the flow of information can cramp this process and leave relationships stagnant.

I'm not suggesting you need to divulge every secret about your life from infancy to adulthood. That's not appropriate behaviour for professional relationships. However, until you engage in something more than the typical, "How are you?" and "What do you do?" banter, you'll find it difficult to truly connect on a substantial level with others.

> **The intensity of a relationship is determined by the quality and depth of information that is shared.**

The intensity of a relationship is not determined by the quantity of information shared between two people, but rather, by the quality and depth of information that is shared. The more intimate the dialogue, the deeper the bond.

Think about what you're willing to share about yourself with a brand new contact compared to what you tell your best friend. There is a big difference on the two ends of the spectrum and there is a variable scale for everyone in between.

A good friend commented that there was just something she didn't trust about a mutual associate. She said, "Something just isn't right." Her observation surprised me, but I was intrigued and open to hear her rationalization for this comment.

She asked if I'd noticed how this contact is totally private about her information, but always wants to know everything about everyone else. It feels like she's on the outside looking in, just collecting information rather than engaging in meaningful conversation.

My friend's perspective made sense. By never sharing her story, this individual did not make it easy for people to know, like or trust her. She did not release any substance about herself, so she came across as having a hidden agenda, which did not endear her to people.

Looking back, I believe one of the reasons I developed such a vast network is because I am willing to share little parts of my life with people I like and with whom I feel I have a connection.

My life is an open book and yes, to add another cliché, I wear my heart on my sleeve. Some would consider it a fault, but from my perspective, this kind of open attitude has made it easier for me to form deeper bonds with many people in a relatively short period of time.

As you increase the number of contacts you make, be prepared to open up so you can change those casual contacts into more important and meaningful relationships in your personal and professional life.

44 Getting and Giving Contact Information

Once you've created a mini-bond and decided you would like to connect with this person again, simply ask for a business card. (Refer to Chapter 47 on How to Exchange Business Cards Properly.)

When you don't have an opportunity to get the card, simply remember who introduced you and ask that person to send you contact details. You can also search the internet for contact information. People who don't carry business cards may suggest you visit their website to touch base with them. If they ask you to contact them, be sure you do.

"

Creating a mini-bond means you've connected enough so the contact will remember you when you follow up or see him the next time.

"

Don't rush to this step of the Mingling Formula. If a mini-bond was not created or there doesn't seem to be a reason to connect in the immediate future, it is not necessary to exchange contact coordinates. This would lead to mere business card collecting.

Not that you want to underestimate your ability to build rapport or you will never get people's contact information. You won't build your network if you don't take a chance by building relationships outside of functions. Creating a mini-bond does not mean that you've become best friends. It's just that you've connected enough so the contact will remember you when you follow up or see him the next time.

If you don't exchange contact details, just take note of anything you discussed. The next time you run into each other mention a tidbit from your last conversation. Your memory of your first encounter will be an instant mini-bond generator.

Sometimes it takes months, or even years, before you actually want to connect with someone in a one-on-one setting. You may see a person every now and again, say hello and ask how he is, but the relationship doesn't go any further than that. Those are your casual contacts and they will stay that way until you find a reason to take the relationship to the next level.

45 Moving On

When I started my company, I had a breakfast meeting with a good friend who is a very successful businessman. I shared my plan for teaching people about business networking and everything the concept entailed.

He laughed and said, "What I need to know is how to end a conversation. The only thing I can think to say when I want to leave the discussion is, 'I have to go to the bathroom.'" I chuckled as I thought, I do see him in hallways going to and from the bathroom – a lot.

As it turns out, exiting a conversation gracefully is the trickiest part of the Mingling Formula, even more so than starting a conversation. People figure once they're in, they're in. To make events worthwhile, you need to talk with multiple people. Learning how to draw a conversation to a close is critical.

For the most part, people don't want to end a conversation because they don't want to appear rude. Well, you're off the hook; the reverse is true. To monopolize someone's time is rude. The general rule of thumb is a maximum of 10 minutes for a conversation between two people at a business function or cocktail party. I'll give you even less. The entire Mingling Formula should happen in three to eight minutes.

Events are opportunities to meet new people and reconnect with current contacts. Thanks to your pre-event homework, you have specific people you hope to meet and others with whom you want to touch base. That can't happen if you spend all night talking with the same person, your best friends and/or co-workers.

> **The entire Mingling Formula should happen in three to eight minutes.**

As an experiment, I once stayed in a corner with one person for an entire function. Naturally, people flowed by and we would engage in dialogue with others, but for several hours it was basically the two of us together. Thankfully, this person was incredibly engaging and we enjoyed our time together. I knew the majority of the people at the conference, so I wasn't concerned about mingling. Halfway through the night I thought, this guy must think no one else wants to talk with me or that I'm a snob and don't want to talk with them.

At the end of the evening, I was even more convinced of the importance of mingling through a room and moving on from conversations. What happened that night was no different than what countless professionals do every time they walk into a room.

The irony is, spending all that time together in a loud room didn't mean that our relationship was much deeper than if we had spent a portion of the time together. It would have made more sense to go to a restaurant and have a real uninterrupted conversation.

Ending a conversation is often a relief for others. Do you really think the other person came to the event to spend his whole night talking with you? Most likely not! Once you get your head around the idea that it is okay to end a conversation, it will make it easier for you to do so without guilt.

There are three likely scenarios that can make it difficult to end a conversation.

1 Both parties would like to end the conversation, but neither knows how.

2 The conversation is really enjoyable and you don't want it to end.

3 Your conversation partner has identified you as a comfort zone and doesn't want you to leave or he will be left alone.

Fortunately, each type of conversation can be ended gracefully with the proper techniques.

There are three ways to exit a conversation:

- The verbal disengage
- The third-party introduction
- The "gotta-go" technique

THE VERBAL DISENGAGE

It's easy to end conversations that fall into Scenarios "1" and "2". Know that it's better to end the conversation on a high note and leave lots to talk about when you reconnect outside of the event. If you hang on too long, you may overstay your welcome. This is a perfect situation for a verbal disengage. Simply have your closing lines ready to end the conversation politely. Some examples of conversation closers are:

- *"I'd like to chat with you more about this. Why don't we grab a coffee sometime outside of this busy event?"* By offering a comment that suggests a reason to meet again somewhere else at another time, the contact will not be offended at all and you've already established a reason to connect later.

- *"Do you have a business card?"* is the perfect way to say, "I'm interested in communicating with you further but our time together at this event has come to an end."
- *"That's great. It was Bill, right?"* Offer a short closing comment that offers validation to the conversation ('That's impressive' or 'No doubt you should be pleased with those results') and then re-establish his name. This is helpful if you didn't catch his name at the beginning.
- *"Well Joe, it's been great talking with you. I'm glad I ran into you."* is a natural closing line that prompts an almost immediate close.

I find this last exit line extremely effective even outside of business functions when you just casually run into people and/or when you want to close a meeting.

Recently a fellow board member and I were having a meeting in the lounge of our dining club. A gentleman who was upstairs attending a private function wandered downstairs and sat in a big comfy lounge chair beside us to join our conversation.

He was a very pleasant man and although we certainly enjoyed the conversation with him, this board member and I had a tight timeframe and pressing issues to discuss. There was no time for anymore idle chitchat.

So I simply offered a, "Well, so and so, am I ever glad you wandered downstairs to say hello. It's been great meeting you." The gentleman returned the sentiment, stood up, shook our hands and with a smile on his face, went back upstairs. It took all of 30 seconds to politely disengage him from our conversation.

Who knows how long the conversation would have continued without my closing statement? I suspect he was equally relieved to have the green light to return to his function.

THE THIRD PARTY INTRODUCTION

The second exit strategy, called the third party introduction, is another great option to close a conversation gracefully. It's especially effective with Scenario "3" when you are speaking with someone who simply doesn't want you to leave. This exit strategy capitalizes on the natural dance that happens as people mingle around a room.

To take advantage of this gracious exit, you simply introduce your contact to another person and once they start their own conversation, you allow them to chat while you begin a conversation with someone new.

"

You have to respect yourself and not allow others to monopolize your time.

"

Third party introductions work best if you are in a high-traffic area. It's tough to have someone casually walk by and join the conversation if you're stuck in, or near, a corner. However, if no one happens to be conveniently nearby, you could suggest that both of you go over to so and so because you would like to introduce her to him.

When Scenario "3" happens, the third party introduction is your best bet because people who are shy or introverted may be concerned that if you leave them, they won't find anyone else to talk with and will be left standing alone.

Don't leave someone hanging, but at the same time, you have to respect yourself and not allow others to monopolize your time. Be kind, but understand that they are not your responsibility.

When you just can't shake someone, it's helpful to know that it's virtually impossible to go to an auction table with a person and leave the auction table with the same person. Inevitably you'll get separated.

THE "GOTTA-GO" TECHNIQUE

As a last resort, you can use the "gotta-go" technique. Chances are you've used this exit strategy before. "I've gotta-go to the auction table, bar, restroom...."

To save your credibility when using this technique, if you say you've "gotta go," then that means you've "gotta go" where you said you were going. It's rather insulting to be left by someone who is supposedly going one place only to see that person head directly somewhere else. Use the "gotta-go" strategy sparingly.

46 Breaking into Group Discussions

Aside from how to exit conversations, the other question I am asked most frequently is how to break into group discussions. Groups can lead to great conversations and new introductions, so it's a worthwhile skill to learn.

The trick to breaking into group discussions is to first notice the dynamics of the group. What is the intensity level? Are two people having a personal conversation? If so, that's not the time to interrupt. Their focus will be on their own issues rather than on getting to know you.

However, if you notice two people together who look disengaged or bored, that's the perfect time to wander over and infuse some energy into their conversation. You will be more than welcome.

It is rude to interrupt two people who are talking and then engage only one of them in dialogue, ignoring the other. When this happens to you, have the social grace to bridge back to the original conversation partner rather than leaving him standing on the outside of the circle.

> **First notice the dynamics of the group. What is the intensity level?**

Look for larger groups having fun. The tone for people to be included is already set. Make eye contact with someone in the group. Most likely he will see your intention to join and open a space for you.

If you are familiar with a group participant, a gentle hand on the person's upper back can let him know you are there and wanting to join. Once a member of the group acknowledges your presence and you have a feel for the group dynamics, offer input into the group discussion.

When you are already part of a group, act as a host or hostess. Always open the circle to others trying to enter. One day they will return the favour. If one person monopolizes the conversation, feel free to ease the transition to another person by shifting the focus from the talker and asking for input from another. "That's quite interesting, Bill. Scott, what do you think?" This will encourage others to participate and feel a part of the group.

When a person enters your group discussion, it's best to finish your current sentence while maintaining eye contact and focus on your original conversation partner(s). Once that thought is complete, then you welcome the newcomer to the group. You might say something such as, "Bob's just telling us about his recent vacation." Then return to the conversation and allow Bob to continue to lead the dialogue.

If the story was complete, you can bridge the conversation by saying something like, "Bob's just told us about his recent vacation. What about you, have you had any travel adventures lately?" This will give the newcomer an opportunity to contribute to the conversation.

As a newcomer to a group, be patient and allow the current sentence to finish. It's awkward when you know someone is waiting in the wings, but then because the conversation didn't come to a grinding halt, they've turned and walked away, probably assuming that you weren't interested in talking with them. A little patience goes a long way in this instance because sooner or later there will be an opening in the conversation.

Group dynamics are constantly shifting. Two or more conversations will naturally spin-off from the original group and mini-groups will form. The sheer nature of the progression of group conversations should eliminate any intimidation entering a group conversation may present to you.

47 Business Cards

Business cards are the single most cost effective marketing tool you can use. It's not about collecting and handing out mass quantities of business cards. The actual cards are just pieces of paper. The real value is the people who are represented by the information on the cards.

Carrying business cards is a no-brainer. Without a business card, how will contacts know how to reach you? It's your calling card for your professional life. They come in lots of 1,000 so use them, but use them wisely.

> **"**
>
> **Business cards are the single most cost effective marketing tool you can use.**
>
> **"**

Among negative networking connotations is the image of a salesman walking into a function and handing out his card randomly to absolutely everyone who walks through the door. What are the chances that those people will call him? Slim to none. In North America, the appropriate exchange of business cards is between two people who have met, had a conversation and created a mini-bond.

At the end of a seminar focused on growing your speaking career, I asked the presenter for her business card. We had spent the day together and I had learned a lot, so I was interested in getting more information. She said she didn't have one.

"Joe," a fellow speaker and author, gave the presenter a knowing nod and said, "Using that old don't-give-'em-your-card-trick, eh?" She smiled. Obviously she knew what trick he meant. I didn't, so I asked.

Turns out, he was referencing the teachings of a networking trainer who teaches business people to *not* hand out their business cards. His theory is that by controlling who gets your card, you can control whom you want to contact and whom you don't.

Wow. I couldn't believe my ears. These are business people who think it's better to keep their business cards in their pocket so they can play gate-keeper before they even know who a person is.

> **"**
>
> **The appropriate exchange of business cards is between two people who have met, had a conversation and created a mini-bond.**
>
> **"**

He defended the position by saying that he follows up if he chooses. Yes, well, I believe that if he receives *and* gives a card he still has the same control. Sure, every now and again you will give your card to a person who will follow up repeatedly and add you to mailing lists without your permission. That's a risk of doing business and that's why you have technology with spam controls.

Imagine the possibilities if you share your card even when you don't feel like it.

What if Joe meets Bill at a conference and after a brief conversation decides not to give out his coveted business card. Joe doesn't "control" the follow-up as he intended to because he gets busy or doesn't see the point in contacting Bill.

Later that week, Bill is enjoying dinner with his wife who happens to be the Human Resources manager for one of Joe's target companies. The wife casually mentions she's pulling together the list of speakers for the company's upcoming sales conference.

Bill says, "Oh, I met a speaker at the conference. The guy who introduced us said he was a really good speaker and he seemed like a nice guy." Wife responds, "Great, I'll check him out. Do you have his contact details?" Bill says, "No, actually I don't. He didn't give me his business card. I gave him my card, but I haven't heard from him since." Wife says, "Oh, too bad." End of story.

Like so many other professionals who don't carry or hand out business cards, Joe thinks that possibility would never happen. How would Joe know? He's too busy trying to grow his business staring at a box of his own business cards.

It's amazing what happens when you make it easy for people to know who you are, what you do and what you have to offer. Crazier stories than the one above have resulted from business card exchanges. That's the beauty of networking. You never know where contacts can lead. Bill's wife has to hire a speaker; we don't know if Joe would have been hired for the job, but at the very least, he would have been considered.

Bottom line: don't prejudge and don't hoard your business cards. Professionals must carry and give business cards. Period.

It is your responsibility to give yourself a chance for success. Not giving business cards either because you forgot them or you want to keep control of your contacts makes it difficult for people to know how to reach you.

At functions, anticipate that people will ask you for your business card. Be prepared. To avoid the unprofessional search or accidental grab of another's card, establish an "inbox" and an "outbox" for your business cards.

" To avoid the unprofessional search or accidental grab of another's card, establish an "inbox" and an "outbox" for your business cards. "

Men, you have it easy – one pocket in, one pocket out. Ladies, buy purses with pockets on the outside so cards are easily accessible with one hand without you having to open your purse. When cards are inside the purse, be sure to organize and minimize the contents of your handbag before the function so contacts don't see a mess.

As stylish as cardholders may look, they are not user-friendly devices at functions. They require two hands to operate – one to open and hold the case and one to remove the card. You have to put down your drink or fumble with your purse while your newest contact watches you go through the awkward exercise with your cardholder. It just adds an unnecessary step that, if eliminated, would add another touch of polish to your image.

In North America, the exchange of business cards happens as an afterthought. In some cultures, the exchange of business cards is a ritual that demands respect. I'd be happy if we could at least meet in the middle.

For starters, slow down the exchange. When you receive a card, actually look at it right away, in front of the person who gave it to you. Read it, notice it, and look at the person again. Who have you just met? Reading the card will help you create a mental snapshot of the person and his name together. Recall the earlier section about remembering names. Business cards, when used properly, can be a huge help in this regard.

The information you just read on the card may spark a question or comment that can lead to a conversation or mutual point of reference. Thank the person for his card and put it into your "inbox."

After the event, empty the cards from your inbox. Write all the details you can remember about each person on the back of the card. When and where did you meet? Who introduced you? What did you discuss? Are there follow-up actions required? Once you have categorized the contact (Refer to Chapter 53 on Categorizing Contacts) you can set the cards aside in your "to enter" box on your desk.

A trick a good friend of mine uses to remember whether further action is required is to dog ear the card or press his fingernail into the card to mark it before he puts it into his pocket. When he reviews his cards after the function, the ones with the indentations or folds go to the priority follow-up pile.

Once a week, personally enter all the new business card contacts into your electronic management system. Include all contact details and all of your notes.

Your reference notes will come in handy in the future when your contact calls. You can have a quick peek and remind yourself where and when you met, what you talked about and who connected you. You will impress the person simply because you cared enough to remember things about him from your initial meeting. This will go a long way to making you likeable.

The beauty of using your business cards in this manner is that it makes you think about your new contact six times:

1   when you were introduced

2   when you accepted his business card

3   when you wrote details on his card

4   when you categorized the contact

5   when you entered his information

6   when you filed the business card

Thinking about contacts after you meet them will help you remember their names and details about them. So often we meet people, but never think about them again. Each time you think about a new contact, you solidify your mental snapshot of that person in your mind.

The process may seem like tedious work, but it takes mere minutes. The benefits gained from these efforts will be longlasting. How do you put a price tag on remembering people? What if remembering that person meant you were able to connect the next time you saw him and he became your client?

Finding a business card system that works for you is imperative to building your ultimate network. The cost of not having a proper system and running the risk of forgetting those you've met is far too great. If you care about building your ultimate network, you have to treat your efforts to connect with people seriously. That means tracking and managing your contacts effectively.

"

Each time you think about a new contact, you solidify your mental snapshot of that person in your mind.

"

48 Communicating YOU: The 5-10-15 Second Communication™

The two most predictable questions that will be asked when you meet someone are, "Do you have a business card?" and "What do you do?"

Unfortunately, these are the two questions that are the most difficult for many professionals to answer appropriately and with confidence. After the last section, hopefully you'll never be caught without a business card again. Now we need to solve the seemingly mysterious second question.

A good friend once said, "If a person can't clearly tell me what he does between 9 and 5 every day, how can he expect me to use his services and trust that he knows what he's doing?" It's a good point. Somewhere along the line the answer to this simple question became complicated.

Remember, it's your responsibility to make it easy for people to know who you are, what you do and what you have to offer. So when you're asked, "What do you do?", you want to establish enough understanding about your deliverables so your contact understands what you do. This is your first opportunity to educate your new contact about what you do and what you have to offer.

Earlier in the book we established that networking is an exercise in education and connection, not sales. That means you do not need to go into a huge sales pitch when asked this question at business functions.

The goal is to establish enough understanding so that when your contacts need your product or service, they will think to call or recommend you first. You want to plant the seed for future, more in-depth business discussions outside of the mingling environment.

People need to understand the basics of what you do and what you have to offer, but they don't need to know every little idiosyncrasy about your company to make the decision to use your services, buy your product or recommend you to someone who will. Once they know the basics, the rest of the decision to do business with you is primarily influenced emotionally, based on whether they like you, trust you and think you're competent. There will be opportunities to communicate more significant information outside of the function, once a potential fit for your services is identified.

You may have heard of the 30-second elevator pitch. It's a popular concept that has you sum up your company in a 30 second commercial. The motivation behind it was that if you found yourself in an elevator face-to-face with a potential investor, you could communicate a summary of your entire business before the elevator ride was finished.

When was the last time you had to promote your company during a short ride in an elevator?

A 30-second elevator pitch is perfect when you need to stand in front of an audience and give a fast blurb about your company. It is also effective when you need to give a synopsis of your company in a more formalized setting such as a sales meeting, introductory phone call or a one-on-one encounter outside of a mingling environment.

> **The concept of a 30-second elevator pitch doesn't make the transition well into real conversations at business functions.**

A solid explanation of your business and your value proposition are expected and appropriate in these situations. In fact, most networking associations dedicate a portion of their formal program for members to share information about their businesses.

Unfortunately, the concept of a 30-second elevator pitch doesn't make the transition well into real conversations at business functions. Most professionals feel they have to compact their entire business into an infomercial. Infomercials exist to sell you something and since networking is not selling, they don't fit.

Your focus is building relationships, finding needs and when there's a fit, moving into the sales process, later, outside of the function. Sales will naturally come from educating people on who you are, what you do and what you have to offer, and from connecting with them positively.

A professional who takes this 30-second, canned approach to answering the "What do you do?" question will lose his conversation partner's interest after about 5 seconds of spewing rhetoric. Halfway through the spiel, the person will be sorry he asked because his attention wanes and his mind drifts to something that's more important to him.

After experiencing a plethora of uncomfortable and/or ineffective answers to this question, I decided there must be a better way for professionals to communicate what they do using a natural conversational approach. Therefore, I developed what I like to call the 5-10-15 Second Communication.

My 5-10-15 Second Communication strategy will keep you from sounding like an infomercial. You still communicate the important details about what you do and what you have to offer, but you do it in a way that is conversational, inviting and natural. It also allows the person who asked the question to be involved in the conversation and saves you from giving a "pitch" to someone who isn't remotely interested in hearing one.

The 5-10-15 Second Communication adapts according to the conversation.

Here's how it works:

Question: What do you do?
Answer: Your 5-second spot presents your **core deliverable**.

Allow your new contact to ask a question or comment on your statement.

Response: Your 10-second spot tells them what they **need** to know so they can understand what you do and a bit about what you have to offer.

Again, allow a question or comment from the person.

Response: Your 15-second spot tells them what they **want** to know.

If the new contact does not make an acknowledging comment or ask a relevant question after you've responded to his opening question with your 5-second spot, then there is no reason to continue to the next step.

To illustrate, here's an example of my 5-10-15 Second Communication.

Question: What do you do?

My 5-second sound bite: *"I do corporate training and consulting on business networking."*

That simple comment will usually prompt a response, either in the form of a comment or a question. This statement will give me the cue to elaborate. If they do not respond in any way that invites further comment from me, I will assume they are not genuinely interested in more information. I realize that sometimes people just ask what you do because they don't know what else to ask.

In that case, they aren't truly interested in the answer to their question. By not responding in a way that invites further comment, they have self-identified as "not interested" in more information. I don't take a lack of response as a personal insult. Not everyone is expected to be interested in my line of work or to need my services.

It's better to save my breath and avoid the "sales pitch" experience. If a person is not interested in more than five seconds of what you have to say, imagine how uncomfortable it would be if you gave a full 30-second explanation of unsolicited information?

Most times you can expect the conversation to go to stage "10." You can usually predict what response will come after the 5-second blurb. In my experience, it's not much. It's often a simple "Oh really?", but it's enough to prompt me to go to the next stage of the dialogue.

My 10-second response communicates what I believe they need to know.

It could sound something like this: *"Yes, I'm working my way onto the speakers' circuit, primarily in the finance sector. Companies hire me to give workshops and keynote talks to train their team on how to make business networking efforts more effective."*

This response changes depending on the flow of conversation, but it's about 10 seconds of information. Within those 10 seconds, there are two key facts I will share:

1   I'm a speaker for hire.

2   I help people become more effective at business networking.

> **"**
>
> **It's about finding their interest in my deliverables and building a conversation around it.**
>
> **"**

This approach is about education versus sales. By this point I've given them enough information that they understand fairly clearly what I do (I train people on business networking) and what I have to offer (I will make them more effective in their networking efforts).

Their response after my 10-second spot will determine the future direction of the conversation. They may simply say, "Cool", which does not solicit any further information. That's fine, my job is complete. I will simply change the subject. If the person chooses to come back to the topic of my business later, we'll talk about it in a more in-depth manner.

On the contrary, if their response after my 10-second spot indicates a desire for more information, I move into my 15-second spot.

The 15-second spot can go in countless directions, depending on the question asked or the comment that was given by the new contact. The 5-10-15 Second Communication allows the flexibility to go with the flow of an effective conversation.

The 15-second spot is less about what I want to communicate and more about what they've asked to know. It's about finding their interest in my deliverables and building a conversation around it.

EXAMPLE 1

Comment: I hear the speakers' industry has a lot of potential.

My 15-second response would talk about the industry and my aspirations for being a part of it. I would allow them to lead the conversation as it interests them. It's about finding common ground in the speakers' industry.

EXAMPLE 2

Comment: We hire speakers for my company all the time.

This is the best-case scenario because the contact has self-identified as a potential client. After the business function, I would move into the sales process with the contact, but for now we're still in networking mode which involves education and connection.

My response in a situation like this would simply be,

"Oh, that's great. Maybe there would be a fit for my training at your company. I would be happy to send you some details and we can go from there."

That's a perfect time to get his business card and end the business talk unless he keeps it going.

If I were to go into a full sales pitch at this point, I would run the risk of over-selling and annoying the person, making him sorry he mentioned his company hires speakers. The person did not attend the function to close a deal with me. I recognize and respect that. The real business discussion is saved for outside of the function.

Once I'm satisfied that there is a potential fit for my services, I will establish that I will follow up in the near future. At this point, strengthening the personal connection becomes the priority. The goal is to be sure the contact remembers me and wants to pick up the phone when I call. It's during the follow-up meeting and through forwarded information that I can communicate the true value I can offer his company.

49 Developing Your Own 5-10-15 Second Communication™

To recap:

- Your 5-second spot is your **core deliverable**.
- Your 10-second spot tells them what they **need** to know.
- Your 15-second spot tells them what they **want** to know.

STEP 1: YOUR 5-SECOND SPOT

What do you do? It's easy to want to sugar coat this answer to create some poetic response to what should be a simple answer. What you do may sound boring, but it's what you do. What makes you appealing is your personality, your value and how you present yourself, not phrases that make your work sound more exciting than it is.

Lines like "It's tough to explain" or "I help people make their dreams come true" or "I help people find the light in the darkness" are too abstract and difficult to understand at functions and make it difficult for others to take you seriously. Put yourself in the other person's shoes. What are comments like that supposed to mean? Are you a top secret agent? Do you work for Disney? Are you an electrician?

Depending on your personality and what your job is, you may be able to get away with an abstract summary about what you do, but for most of us, it's best to be up front and honest.

Whatever your profession, you'll appear more successful if you are clear and confident as you communicate what you do. Hiding behind fluffy phrases will project a sense that you're withholding something or ashamed of what you do. As an investment advisor, you need to educate contacts that you're an investment advisor. Not clearly communicating this fact will make it difficult for people who need an investment advisor to choose you or refer you to others who do. The same requirement applies regardless of your profession.

A client expressed concern that people want to run away from him when they find out he sells insurance. Many people have told me they feel the same way about their profession. In my client's case, the reality is, at some point, the people he's interacting with will need insurance. Since he specializes in a specific field, it is likely they could purchase insurance from him. Not letting people know he's in insurance will keep them from being able to buy insurance from him because they won't understand what he does and what he has to offer.

His fear can be overcome by presenting a genuine, welcoming professional image that encourages people to want to interact with him on a personal level. Not trying to "sell" them insurance on the spot, but rather focusing on making authentic connections will dispel any potentially negative image associated with a certain industry or profession.

> *Step 1: Determine your core deliverable. In a nutshell, what do you do?*

MY 5-SECOND SPOT

_____

_____

_____

STEP 2: YOUR 10-SECOND SPOT

What does someone *need* to know about you to decide to buy your product or use your services? What seeds need to be planted to give a blue-sky perspective of your professional value?

Again, your 10-second communication shouldn't be complicated. It needs to be clear and easy to understand. When formulating your response, brainstorm ideas that need to be communicated. Then formulate them into point-form notes. Know the general gist of what you need to say and then let the sentences form naturally when you're in a conversation. This approach is more effective than blurting out a canned speech. It is vitally important to make your 10-second spot as simple as possible.

In my 5-10-15 Second Communication example, I've given enough information and planted enough of a seed so that when my contact needs to hire a speaker or is complaining about networking not being effective, it will trigger a thought that says, "I think that's what Allison does; maybe she can help us."

What are the two most important things people need to know about what you do?

POINTS FOR MY 10-SECOND SPOT

1 _____

_____

2 _____

_____

STEP 3: YOUR 15-SECOND SPOT

This is your opportunity to prove you are competent. Listen to the comments made or questions asked and answer them openly and honestly. Be flexible with the direction in which the person wants to take the conversation. Limit yourself to 15 second answers. Don't go on endlessly or they'll regret asking you to expand on the topic.

If you know your stuff (and you should because you live it daily), answering these questions and responding to any comments should be easy. As soon as you've identified that a person is interested in your product or service, acknowledge intentions to follow up. Resist the urge to go into sales mode and focus on building the relationship.

If you haven't already done so, now is a good time to switch the emphasis from you to your contact. Get him talking and sharing.

Again, *perspective*, *preparation* and *practice* are paramount to delivering a solid 5-10-15 Second Communication and successfully educating others as to who you are, what you do and what you have to offer.

PERSPECTIVE

When someone asks you what you do, they are not looking for a long-winded, in-depth answer. They just need to know enough to decide if they want to know more. Your connection could come from a topic that is not work related, so getting too hung up on being sure contacts know everything about your work could stifle your ability to find common ground in other areas that are more interesting to them.

Allow time for the relationship to build. Eventually they may need your services or know someone who does and that's when they'll get all the "goods" about what you have to offer.

PREPARATION

When you know the key messages you need to communicate, you will be able to formulate naturally flowing conversations around these bullet points.

PRACTICE

The more you communicate who you are, what you do and what you have to offer, using my 5-10-15 Second Communication, the easier and more effective you will become at communicating YOU.

50 General Business Etiquette

GRAMMAR AND SPELLING

"c u l8r." is not a sentence. "See you later." is. Texting has become the norm of the day. These short forms, used by the masses under the age of 30, are replacing acceptable written and verbal communication skills. As a young professional who wants to connect with more established professionals, leave these short forms for communiqués with your best friends and take a refresher course on proper English.

> **"**
> **Don't underestimate the power of proper grammar as you build your personal brand.**
> **"**

Starting a conversation with "Yo! Whazs Up?" creates a completely different gut feeling about a person than, "Hello, how are you?" To be taken seriously as a professional, using the second phrase would be more impressive than the first.

Calling people "Girl", "Hon", "Sweetie", "Babe", "Dude" etc. is not appropriate when addressing others in business settings. Make sure all of your professional interactions are just that – professional.

Don't underestimate the power of proper grammar as you build your personal brand.

When you communicate with others in the business realm through writing, use spell and grammar check features on your computer and a dictionary, if needed, to check spelling for your handwritten notes.

EMAILS

The easier you make it for people to get in touch with you, the more likely they will. A great way to do that is to make your contact details highly visible on all communication.

A full electronic signature including your name, company, mailing address, phone number, fax number, website, and email address should be on the bottom of every email you send, including replies and emails sent from your mobile device. It's a simple courtesy that can make it easy for people to copy you into their electronic address books, find your number when it's better to answer via the telephone, or locate your office address when they are running late for a meeting.

"Signatures" only take you a few minutes to set up, but will save your contacts time because they won't have to hunt for ways to reach you. Not everyone inputs data into an address book so if you don't send your contact details, they may not have them handy. I've actually given up trying to respond to people when it becomes too time-consuming to track down their contact information.

Forwarding jokes and chain emails should be saved for friends, not for business associates. Having time to forward these notes sends a message that you're not very busy at work. If an email is particularly funny or has a certain relevance to a particular contact, send him a targeted forward, not an email to your entire distribution list.

> **Whenever you send something via email, it is permanently "out there" in cyberspace.**

Emotions are very difficult to communicate via email. If an issue requires sensitivity, pick up the phone instead of sending the message via email. Keep in mind that whenever you send something via email, it is permanently "out there" in cyberspace. It can be forwarded to anyone or read by the wrong person. It only takes one negative incident to make a person leery of email security.

Keep an eye on your spam folder. Many a message has been lost thanks to overzealous spam filters. If you don't hear back from a contact, and the email required a response, then wait an appropriate amount of time to make a follow-up call.

Before following up on non-urgent emails, allow three to seven days, including a weekend, as a courtesy for people to catch up on their messages. The person could be swamped or perhaps your message was filtered through spam and wasn't delivered. When you call to inquire about the response, don't put the contact on the defensive by accusing him of ignoring your email or even subtly suggesting this has happened.

Simply say, "I wanted to follow up by telephone just in case you didn't receive my initial email." He will likely apologize and mention his hectic schedule. Respond by empathizing and hopefully, you will get the required details at that time.

Use the blind carbon copy or BCC function on your email whenever you send group emails, unless you are expecting people to "Reply All". It's inconsiderate to send someone's email address to an entire group. Although they shouldn't, anyone who has a blast email distribution list could copy those addresses for their own use.

TELEPHONE COMMUNICATION

The world of technology has eliminated a lot of telephone communication. Often you'll find yourself leaving a voicemail rather than connecting with a live person.

From a time management perspective, it takes longer to listen to voicemails and return calls than it does to answer a phone call on the first ring. Set a standard to return voicemails within a set timeframe. Responding within 24 hours or by the end of the business day are good rules to adopt. Doing this shows respect for others.

When you leave a voicemail, be sure to state your name and telephone number slowly and clearly. Leave your name and number once at the onset of the message and again at the close of the message. That way, the listener has a second chance to write your number and he can hear it again without listening to the entire message twice.

It's also important to tell the person why you're calling. That will give him a heads-up to prepare for the return call because he understands the urgency of the situation and the approximate length of time required.

Depending on the nature of the voicemail you leave, it may be a different person who returns your call. Executives will often have their assistant call to arrange the meeting. The assistant will only call you if the executive has agreed to meet with you, so don't be offended; it's just an effective way for him to manage time.

Messages that play hard to get or leave a mystery as to why you're calling lack professionalism. When you're networking well, the person on the receiving end will be happy to take your call, even if it's to say he can't help you.

I'm a big fan of the voicemail that tells them you'll send an email in case that's an easier option for them to respond to you. That way, you've taken the extra step to make the phone call, but still you've offered the ease of responding through email.

A typical voicemail from me to a prospective client would be:

"Hi, so and so, this is Allison Graham calling, 519-555-1212. As we discussed at last week's event, I'm just touching base to discuss a potential fit for my services with your company. I will send you an email with some available dates in case that's an easier way for us to connect. Again, it's Allison Graham, 519-555-1212. I look forward to hearing from you either by email or telephone."

The follow-up email reads,

"As promised on your voicemail, I am sending you some available dates to meet to discuss a potential fit for my services. (insert dates here) are still open. Hopefully one of these dates will work for you. If not, please let me know some alternative dates so we can go from there. Thanks!"

Phrases like "as promised" and "just following up" subtly communicate that you are trustworthy and follow through on your commitments. Delivering the little things will slowly, but surely, earn you a reputation as someone who is credible and competent.

If it's a quick fact that needs to be communicated, like "The dress code for tomorrow's dinner is black tie," then simply leave this information on the voicemail. Leaving a message that says, "Give me a call and I'll let you know about the dress code for tomorrow night" generates more back and forth activity than busy people can handle. If you can, close the loop on the call and avoid telephone tag.

The key to using the phone effectively is to respect the other person. Long phone conversations should be reserved for family and friends, not business associates.

> **"**
>
> **It's better to deal with the business up front and naturally broach the personal questions to find common ground as the call progresses.**
>
> **"**

When you do connect live with a person over the phone, be aware of his tone. You can tell when the person on the other end of the line is in a rush. Forcing the person to exchange pleasantries could annoy him, especially when it's obvious his time is limited and he just needs to hear the bare facts from you.

Hearing a stark hello on the other end of the telephone line usually means the conversation should get to the point. Asking about the family and how everyone is enjoying the weather will likely frustrate your listener in these cases more than it will establish rapport.

You have no way of knowing what a person is doing when you call on the phone. He could be walking into a meeting, in the middle of handling a crisis or sitting at his desk playing solitaire because of boredom. Listen for clues and mirror your contact's pace as best you can.

It's better to deal with the business up front and naturally broach the personal questions to find common ground as the call progresses. When you engage in extended pleasantries at the beginning of the phone conversation, the person on the other end may wonder why you're calling. Give that information right away.

It's always safe to ask, "Did I catch you at an okay time?". I recommend this phrase rather than, "Did I catch you at a bad time?" because realistically, until you know this person well enough and he makes the decision that he wants to talk with you, if he's busy, any time you call will probably be a bad time. Until the person decides he wants to make time to talk with you, the best that you can hope for is to catch him at an okay time.

Be sure to smile when you use the phone. A person can hear a smile.

CONFERENCE CALLS

Conference calls are popular and time efficient ways to communicate with several people at once. As a word of caution, unless you are speaking, activate your mute button. It's distracting when you hear all the multi-tasking that's happening in the background. Covering the phone with your hand while talking with someone else, coughing, going to the facilities or typing on your computer is not enough. It can all be heard by others on the conference call unless your phone is muted.

MOBILE DEVICES

Mobile devices are great conveniences of our time as well as great distractions. As difficult as it is to lose touch with the outside world, turn off your cell phone and email capabilities while you're at business functions. You're not hiding anything by doing the "Blackberry prayer" under the table. Everyone knows you're typing a message to someone outside of the room. Focus on the present moment and connect with the people who are in front of you.

SOCIAL NETWORKING SITES

Websites such as *My Space* and *Facebook* are quite popular among young professionals. They are also popular among Human Resource professionals and potential clients who want to find out about you. Take special note of what you're posting on the World Wide Web. Once it's posted, it's there forever. If you wouldn't want your new boss or client to see it, don't post it. Inappropriate materials have a way of catching up with people eventually.

PROFESSIONAL NETWORKING SITES

As for professional networking sites, I know there are people who use them and have found success with them. The best use I've found for online networking is to reconnect with people already in my network.

> **I'm not convinced technology can take the place of those in-person experiences and connections.**

I admit to not being a fan of networking sites, mainly because my philosophy on developing the ultimate network is focused on the realm of "high-touch" versus "high-tech." My personal network came from meeting people face-to-face and, while it plays a myriad of useful roles in our lives, I'm not convinced technology can take the place of those in-person experiences and connections.

Call me old-fashioned, but being linked electronically doesn't necessarily mean I will do business with people. How do you know if you like them, trust them or think they are competent? Anyone can be anything online. Yes, people can pretend to be anything in person too, but at least when you have an in-person encounter you have a reference point from which to form an opinion. You have the natural warning signs, body language and gut feelings that are generated through your interaction. That's not the case online.

No doubt technology can support relationship development and lead to new acquaintances. My concern is you could have 10,000 contacts in a database, but if you don't have actual relationships with those people, then they are not really part of your ultimate network. These lists are great assets for semi-cold and cold calls plus direct mailing programs as well as advertising, but not for true business networking.

TIMELINESS

Time is money. So, wasting people's time is equivalent to wasting their money. Earning a reputation as the person who is always late is not desirable. It sends the message that you are disorganized and that you disrespect other people and their time.

Be sure to schedule enough time in between appointments to accommodate the unexpected. Jamming too much into too short a period of time can run you ragged and make you less effective.

As a courtesy when running late, call or email the person to let him know you'll be delayed in getting to the meeting. For those who don't have access to mobile devices, notify them by calling their receptionist or the restaurant where you're supposed to meet.

If you are going to be late by 10 minutes or more, you definitely have to call to keep your contact from wondering if you've forgotten. After waiting for 15 minutes, without notification of your late arrival, it is acceptable for your contact to leave.

SCHEDULING AND CANCELLING APPOINTMENTS

Whenever possible, cancel appointments a minimum of 48 hours in advance. Professionals who live by their calendar would have scheduled other appointments and possibly travel plans around your agreed-upon meeting time. Notify the other person as soon as you realize you are no longer available at that time. Whenever possible, stick to the time that was scheduled.

HOW TO SAY NO WITHOUT BURNING A BRIDGE

For a word we hear so often in our lives, "NO" is a very difficult word to say when we're asked to do something, especially in the professional realm. Saying "YES" all the time means you're going to run out of time and energy, which are limited resources.

The worst way to say no is to not respond to requests. It's unprofessional to leave someone hanging, hoping he will conclude that because you're ignoring him, you're not interested. You'll feel uncomfortable the next time you see the person and rightly so. To ignore someone is just short of being ignorant.

> **To ignore someone is just short of being ignorant.**

People are adults. Sure they may be disappointed, but their world will not crumble if you do not join the committee, come over for dinner or buy their product.

The first step in learning how to say NO is to decide when you want to say YES. Activities that fit your focus board (Refer to Chapter 59 on The Focus Board) make great "yes" opportunities. Decide if you have the time and financial resources to follow through and if so, great. Say, "Yes."

If the answer must be no, here is a simple way to say no without offending others.

This example would be useful if you were asked and weren't able to join a board of directors or committee. If this doesn't match your personality, use the premise of this technique, but tone it down so it is genuine for you and applicable to your situation.

"Am I ever flattered, honoured in fact, that you would think of me for such an important role. That being said, after looking at my calendar and considering my current work and family commitments, I know I wouldn't do the role justice. I would hate to say yes, then not deliver. I'd make you look bad for recommending me. I hope you understand and can respect this decision."

You can also add (but only if it is truthful and applies to the situation): *"Even though I am not able to assist in an official capacity, by all means, please keep me posted if there are upcoming events. I would be happy to buy a ticket or make a donation to support such a worthwhile cause."*

You could also offer a recommendation in case the person doesn't know who else to ask. You could say, *"I wonder if so and so would be in a better position to help you in this case. If you'd like, I'd be happy to make the introduction."*

Now, if someone is asking you to sponsor him for a run, something this elaborate would not be necessary, but if you really don't wish to sponsor this person for any reason, take elements from this technique to politely say no. A simple, "Unfortunately, I've already allocated my resources for this year." will suffice.

MEETINGS

Before any meeting, challenge yourself to determine if your attendance at the meeting is really necessary. Meeting-happy cultures within organizations can develop very quickly and can zap productivity.

> **Meeting-happy cultures within organizations can develop very quickly and can zap productivity.**

If you are the one in charge of calling the meeting, don't have a meeting just for the sake of having a meeting. Make sure that before you ask others to attend, you have a full, substantial agenda and that you are only inviting those who have a direct concern with the topics being discussed. Be clear and honest about the intention for the meeting so attendees can decide if it's a worthwhile time investment for them to attend.

There are few meetings that require longer than one hour to complete the agenda. If you find meetings are lasting longer, there may be too much focus on *doing* the work rather than *deciding* what work needs to be done and then *delegating* accordingly.

Before you speak at a meeting, jot a list of the points you would like to make on a piece of paper. That will help you avoid pontificating. It's difficult for people to like you when you're holding up the meeting just to hear yourself talk. Short, sweet and right-to-the-point comments make for effective meeting control.

As the chair of a meeting, take time to learn techniques that will ensure meetings are respectful of attendees and their time.

CLOSING THE LOOP

When a person makes a recommendation or connects you with an individual, close the loop on the situation. Just a quick note, such as the following will work: "Thanks for connecting me with so and so. We're going to meet on Monday to see if there is potential to collaborate." or "Thanks for the recommendation; she's a great accountant."

Tying up loose ends shows respect to the person who opened and shared his network with you. On a few occasions when I've set people up with potential employers, I didn't find out they got the job until months later. A quick update with the happy news would have gone a long way to solidifying our professional relationship.

It's also professional to keep people updated on progress if they've offered you assistance and/or support, whether it's sponsoring a cause, cheering you on as you look for work or mentoring you as you start your career.

SHOWING APPRECIATION

When someone goes above and beyond general expectations for you, it's only polite to thank him. Actually, whenever anyone does anything for you, it's appropriate to give thanks. The situation will dictate what should be done – use your judgement and match your personality. I often meet with young professionals to help them get connected. I am happy to do this and genuinely enjoy meeting new people. In fact, time permitting, I rarely turn down a first meeting with anyone who asks. This is an attitude I've chosen to guide my networking efforts and I would encourage anyone who is looking to build the ultimate network to follow suit. You never know with whom you will connect and where that connection could lead.

Every now and again, I'll meet with young professionals who act as if picking my brain and accessing my professional network are things they're entitled to. I've talked with others who have noticed an increase in the same kind of attitude. This sense of entitlement is not appropriate because it does not encourage long-term, mutually beneficial business relationships.

After several attempts to connect one person with various employers, I realized that not once did he offer a simple thank you. In fact, each time I updated him on my efforts on his behalf, he simply asked for another favour and another connection. Despite his qualifications and positive in-person impression, his behaviour deterred me from helping him further.

Failing to thank someone is a surefire way to stop the development of a relationship. Conversely, those who offer sincere appreciation make you feel good about helping them.

A handwritten thank-you card is a lost art form, but one that is always noticed and appreciated. When people have made a tremendous impact on my life, I will opt to send them a gift basket that supports a local charitable cause.

When attending a dinner party at someone's home, it is appropriate to bring a host or hostess gift. A bottle of wine or flowers will suffice. Visit a specialty store for more unique hostess gifts if it's a special occasion or you would like to stray from the norm. A follow-up thank-you call within 48 hours of a dinner party is a minimum pleasantry and a follow-up thank-you note is always appreciated.

ALCOHOL

Know your limits. As much as you may think you can handle alcohol, it affects the brain's normal functioning. There are many business deals that have gone sideways thanks to an inappropriate comment made due to the influence of alcohol. Just because other people choose to drink does not give you the green light to do the same. It's better to stay in control than to risk doing something you'll regret.

Limit alcohol to one or two drinks in public. Getting drunk will not earn you points in the professional realm. DO NOT drink and drive. Not only is this just a good personal policy, getting behind the wheel after drinking is irresponsible and inconsiderate and will detract from your credibility. The price of a taxi is nothing compared to the potential damage mixing alcohol and driving could cause.

↗ Section 3 Summary

- Mastering the fundamentals of networking will add to your professional image and give you confidence.

- Know the Mingling Formula – initiate dialogue, create a mini-bond, get and/or give contact information, move on and repeat often.

- Do not be intimidated by the start of a conversation, but rather, be prepared to confidently engage in dialogue.

- Don't underestimate the power of pre-event planning. A game plan for attendance at an event will give you purpose so you can maximize your time.

- You will have a better chance to achieve your ultimate network if you have the support and understanding of your family, friends and co-workers. Educate your significant others about your goals and the path required to succeed.

- Make the most of your time at networking functions. Consider your cost for being in the room and be sure you are getting your money's worth.

- You don't have to be a social butterfly to make group environments worthwhile. Whatever your personality, you can tailor techniques to your comfort zone to maximize your time investment.

- The attitude you bring to an event is as important as what you do when you are there.

- Dining should be an enjoyable experience, not only for you, but for everyone around you as well. Do all you can to ensure you are considerate of others.

- Forgetting a name is not the end of the world. It happens. Relax. Make a conscious effort to remember names by using the **Listen**, **Solidify** and **Think** strategy.

- Accept the fact that people may forget your name. Kindly offer your first and last name to new and reacquainted contacts to ease the pressure of them trying to figure out who you are.

- A name tag should include your first and last names as well as company name. It should then be placed high on your right shoulder.

- Your handshake is the subconscious communication of your character. Every handshake counts.

- Adopt a business card system that works for you. Show respect when accepting cards by reading the information in front of the person who gave it to you.

- Creating mini-bonds is vital to networking. Without mini-bonds, connections won't deepen.

- Make a conscious effort to become an effective listener.

- Develop your own 5-10-15 Second Communication so you can effectively answer the question "What do you do" in a mingling situation.

Section 4
The Strategy

51 Now what?

Y ou have dealt with the Business of YOU. You are confident. You have learned the fundamentals of business networking and are well equipped to present a professional, put-together image.

Now what? Where do you go? Who do you need to meet? How do you take the Business of YOU and create the ultimate network?

The truth behind building the ultimate network is that regardless of how professional and polished your image and how well you know the fundamentals, if you aren't meeting new people and building relationships, you're not going to grow your network. Talking about networking and actually networking are two different things.

It is amazing how people will say they want to build their network, but then a month later they still haven't made an effort to get to know even one new contact.

Bottom line: If you want to expand your network, then you have to network.

Networking takes work. As we established earlier, it takes six months or as many as six to eight casual contacts with others before you hit their radar screen and they start to "get" who you are. Expect it to take about 12 to 18 months of consistent and persistent effort to solidify the foundation for your ultimate network.

There are two ways to approach networking. The first is to use the "throw-mud-on-the-wall-and-hope-some-of-it-sticks" method that is seemingly quite popular. The second option is to be strategic about your efforts so you can put yourself in the best position to win.

With limited time and money, the second option is the obvious choice. Many professionals run themselves ragged spinning their wheels and wondering why networking doesn't work for them. A proactive plan is the key to avoid feeling that way.

The most likely starting point to build your ultimate network is to analyze your current network and figure out who you already know.

"

Talking about networking and actually networking are two different things.

"

Imagine that for every day you're alive, you've crossed paths with three new people. Some days more, some days less, but as difficult as it may be to believe, it's about right. For easy numbers, let's round down to 1,000 new interactions per year. For a professional who is working outside of the home, this is a low estimation.

By that calculation, if you are 33 years old, you have encountered approximately 33,000 people. Someone 55 years old would have encountered 55,000 people and so on. Chances are you'd have a tough time naming that many people, but surely you can name a hundred right off the top of your head, even if you are an 18 year old hermit.

If you have networked for years, or if you're brand new to the concept, chances are you already have a solid base of contacts available to jumpstart your networking efforts. You may just not realize it. Think of your friends, your family, your family's friends, your work colleagues or your teammates as a start.

Those of you who are not already using a data management system should start by compiling a list of everyone you know into one accessible electronic tracking system. As you gather these names, don't restrict who goes on the master list. Think about the number of people you've met in your lifetime. For how many of these contacts could you find phone numbers, plus street or email addresses with a moment's notice? If the answer is not many, this activity will change that.

Once your master list is complete, review it. Ask yourself, "How can my current network help me achieve my goals and aspirations? Have I attracted the kind of people that I want into my life?"

By simply taking time to consider your list and your current circles of influence, you may notice a pattern. Are you surrounding yourself with people who influence you positively or negatively?

> **"**
>
> **Are you surrounding yourself with people who influence you positively or negatively?**
>
> **"**

Next, check your list to find the most successful person on it. Does this successful person know you too? If yes, that's great! This is where and with whom your official business networking efforts will begin.

Put a smile on your face and call that person. Let him or her know you want to get more involved in the community or that you are looking for a new job. Perhaps you have just started a new job and want to build your network.

Whatever your needs are, be up front about your intention for making the contact and setting the meeting. It may help if you say, *"You're the most successful person I know, so I thought I would start by calling you. I'm really hoping to build my business network. I would be interested to hear how you got started."*

There are many reasons to start your networking plan with the most successful person you know. It will stretch you out of your comfort zone early in the process and therefore, make all of your subsequent networking efforts easier.

Establishing yourself with the movers and shakers from the beginning will give you credibility and start your networking efforts on a positive note. As you build your network, you will want and need to find a mentor who will take you under his wing to help you get established.

It could very well be this first person you call, but don't be discouraged if it's not. Finding the right fit for a mentor can be a process all on its own.

Surround yourself with people who have achieved what you want to achieve. This way you'll be motivated, mentored and ready to succeed. You can't learn how to become successful from someone who is unsuccessful.

> **You can't learn how to become successful from someone who is unsuccessful.**

When you call your most successful person of choice, it's important to already have a connection with him through a mutual friend or family member. It is actually best if you've met personally before. That way, when you call, he will have a reference point for who you are and will be happy to speak with you. Hopefully, he will point you in the right direction to help you start your networking process.

If your relationship is strong enough to go for lunch or breakfast, then ask for that. If not, ask to meet for 15 to 20 minutes maximum, so the timeline is short and convenient. Let him know you would like to learn how to create success and emulate what he has done. This tells him the purpose of the meeting and it gives him an opportunity to agree to it or not. Make sure you respect the time limit by not staying longer than you promised.

When you meet, be on time and be prepared. Be honest and open about your ideal vision as determined in Chapter 2. Ask questions and seriously listen to the answers. Take a pen and paper to write brief notes.

Let the conversation flow. You will learn more by listening than by talking. After all, he's the expert and you are the student. Know in advance what you want to learn during this meeting and prepare some relevant questions. However, avoid turning the meeting into an interrogation interview.

It's natural to be a little nervous when you're sitting in front of the one you deem to be the most successful person you know, but remember, this person has already agreed to meet with you. Relax and enjoy the experience. Appreciate the opportunity to pick his brain.

As you build your network, and especially in these mentorship type settings, there are two vital questions that will help you expand your network:

1 Where should I go?

2 Whom should I meet?

Asking contacts these questions will give you the direction you need to connect the dots to create your ultimate network.

For example, imagine you're a young professional who wants to find a job in the technology sector. You call the most successful person you know who just happens to be the gentleman whose lawn you cut all the way through high school. He is the chief executive officer of an oil and gas company.

You did a great job for him all those years, so he already perceives you as reliable. You walk into the meeting presenting a professional image. You're prepared, punctual and looking polished in your tidy suit.

At your meeting, you explain your ideal job and the type of company you want to work for in the technology sector. You ask, "Is there anywhere you think I should go and/or anyone you think I should meet?"

Mr. CEO ponders for a moment and calls his colleague to ask what technology show it was that she mentioned her husband was going to on the weekend. He explains to her that he has a young man sitting in his office who is looking for a job in technology.

Since the CEO and this lady have a positive relationship through networking, she trusts his judgement and she agrees to introduce you to her husband who happens to own a technology company. He may not be hiring, but at least you will gather information about the technology show and he can introduce you to others who are potentially hiring.

That's how networking can work, but to make a ripple effect like that happen, you need to take responsibility to identify and approach people you perceive to be successful and potentially significant in your life so you can ask the key questions. If you don't ask, people won't think to give you the answers.

You can repeat the process with more than one person, but start with the most successful choice and then work towards your honourable mentions.

There is no limit to the number of times you can use this approach to make connections. However, each time follow these six equally important rules:

> **If you don't ask, people won't think to give you the answers.**

1 Contact people with whom you already have a connection, either on your own or through a mutual contact.

2 Respect their time: keep your meetings brief, be prepared and be clear about your intentions.

3 Follow up on their suggestions, otherwise their time was wasted. Lack of follow-up is the most common mistake professionals make.

4 Don't pressure them to connect you with their network on the spot. Recognize that some professionals aren't as forthcoming when it comes to sharing their contacts – and rightly so. They've spent years building trusting relationships and expanding their circles of influence. That should not be taken lightly.

5 Thank them for the time spent with you. Remember, people don't have to meet with you; they choose to.

6 Keep them posted on your progress, especially if the good news you have to share is a result of their guidance.

There you have it – your first step in building your ultimate network. Connect with the most successful person(s) you know and see where these connections lead you. Even if you've been networking for a while, this is a great way to boost your network to the next level.

52 Electronic Filing System

To tap into your professional network, information about your contacts needs to be easily accessible. This requires an electronic filing system. Grandma-style paper address books won't cut it in today's competitive world.

A client prided herself on her business card filing system. She had hundreds of cards filed alphabetically in a leather-bound business card book. I agreed that her system looked very impressive.

During a consulting session, she mentioned her plans to contact a certain fellow when the company was ready to open its next satellite office. It was a commendable plan, but when asked about the contact she couldn't remember his name, only the country where he lived. After flipping through pages of business cards, she found a card she thought might be his, but she wasn't sure.

If this client had been using an electronic filing system and had included all pertinent details in the notes section, she simply could have searched for her potential contact by referencing his country and the project name. In a matter of seconds, her computer would have produced a short list of people from his country who were associated with the project.

> **"**
>
> **To tap into your professional network, information about your contacts needs to be easily accessible.**
>
> **"**

This client gets bonus points for making an effort to organize her business cards because often professionals will not organize them at all. It's normal for me to visit offices where I see stacks of business cards tied with elastic bands or cards thrown randomly in a desk. These systems – or lack thereof – will not allow for effective relationship management.

There's a difference between having a bunch of business cards and having a strong network of meaningful contacts with easily accessible contact information.

Those of you who have not been tracking contacts electronically have a big task ahead of you. If you did not complete your master list of contacts when it was suggested in the last chapter, now is the time to compile all of their information into one database.

Those who type slowly or who lack the time to input the data should hire someone to do it for you. It will be money well spent. Most programs will import data from spreadsheet programs so you do not even need to give up your computer for the day.

Regardless of which program you use, you'll want to track all pertinent details about each contact. The cell phone, a popular electronic storage device, is not a substitute for a real contact management system.

Chances are, until reading this book, you haven't written notes on the back of your cards. If you have, kudos to you; you're one step ahead of the pack. (Refer to Chapter 47 on How to Use Business Cards Properly.) Always be sure to include those special notes into your electronic filing system.

I wish I had learned that trick when I started networking. There are countless people whom I've met along the way, yet I have no idea how to reach them now, nor do I remember how we met. It wasn't until a couple of years ago that I realized the unequivocal importance of a system to track contacts.

Once all your business card information is entered into your data system, proceed to the next chapter to categorize your contacts.

53 Categorizing Contacts

To tap into the power of networking, you must first be aware of who is in your network. You've just made a master list of everyone you know. Now figure out where those people fit in your professional life.

A client had close to 750 names in his electronic database yet he insisted he didn't have anywhere to start his networking and business development efforts. So I asked him to review and categorize all 750 names.

At our next meeting, the number of his legitimate contacts dropped to almost 150. The other 600 names were of people he didn't know. They were mostly the result of cold calls he made at the start of his investment career. Some were random business cards he'd entered, but couldn't remember anything about the people represented by the cards, so they weren't considered meaningful contacts.

> **The more people you have in your database, the more important it is to organize your current network.**

The exercise gave us a manageable place to start. In addition to eliminating all the people who weren't really contacts, the exercise identified priority prospects with whom he'd forgotten to follow up concerning their investment portfolios.

The more people you have in your database, the more important it is to organize your current network. Otherwise it will be difficult to grasp the complexity of your network and tap into it effectively.

As you review your current list and add new contacts to it, you'll want a system that allows you to categorize each contact easily. Without an easy-to-use system, you run the risk of just collecting names, rather than keeping them organized enough to generate long-term mutually beneficial business relationships.

The more straightforward you make your contact categorization system, the more likely you will be to follow it. My system is a simple 1, 2, 3 – it doesn't get much easier than that.

1 General Contacts

2 Connectors

3 Target Market

This system helps determine action steps for further connection and ongoing relationship management.

For those involved in multiple projects, subcategories within each of the three categories may be helpful to track people who apply to different industries or projects in which you're involved.

Choosing too many categories can make your database too complicated, thereby making it difficult to implement on an ongoing basis. The idea is to make a fast judgement about the next steps for follow-through and relationship management for each contact. If you only have three categories in your database system, a decision as to where the card belongs becomes easy, fast and accurate for successful retrieval when needed.

1. GENERAL CONTACTS

These are the people you meet, but who don't seem to have a specific place in your professional network yet or an immediate connection was not established. They are not identified as potential clients nor has a specific reason to follow up been identified.

People in the general category will likely form the bulk of your database. Keep notes about each person as we discussed in previous chapters. I often look to my "general contacts" to connect other people with services.

These contacts are as important to track as those in the next two categories because you never know what the future may hold. People who start in your database as general contacts may change categories as your paths cross and circumstances evolve.

2. CONNECTORS

For me, as will be the case for you, these contacts are the pulse of my network. Our personalities click. We share common goals and perhaps we plan to collaborate on a project.

These are the movers and shakers of the present or possibly the future. Connectors are happy to connect others and happy to connect with you. They are part of your circle of influence and create the core of your business network.

Perhaps your services are complementary and sending referrals to each other seems likely. Developing relationships with people in Category 2 is enjoyable because you like them, trust them and believe they are competent and vice versa. As well, these relationships could prove to be professionally advantageous and profitable someday.

Focus on the long-term relationships with this group. Think of the connectors as individuals you won't necessarily do business with today (although you may), but as the people who will lead you to business tomorrow.

3. TARGET MARKET

"

As circumstances evolve, general contacts and connectors may become part of your target market category.

"

These are the people who have been identified or who have identified themselves as potential clients. They need timely follow-up and should move to the top of your priority list to start the sales process. As circumstances evolve, general contacts and connectors may become part of your target market category.

These categories can be especially handy when you go to fill your calendar with networking opportunities. You can pull a list of names from

Category 2 to see who you should connect with over the course of the next month. When you do your pre-event homework, you may consider the people from your categorized contacts who will most likely be in the room.

At times when you are looking to book sales meetings, you can pull a list of prospects from Category 3 and take appropriate steps to move them closer to actual clients.

As you meet new contacts, it will take less time to monitor and categorize where they fit into your network. If you categorize contacts automatically when you get a new business card and keep up to date with inputting data, this process will happen very quickly and smoothly. Add a "category" tab to your electronic database so contacts can be easily sorted and managed according to your categories.

> *Once you've established the categories you'll use to manage your contacts, print a master list of your current contact management database. One by one, go through the list to assign a 1, 2 or 3 to each contact. During this process consider the needs of those in your network.*

What is happening in their lives right now? Are they buying a new car or a new home? When you listen to and actually think about the people you know, you'll be surprised how much information about them you have already stored in your head.

As you perform this exercise, you may find natural connections. For example, you may know that your friend Sue is looking for a new babysitter and that Sandra's daughter just finished her babysitting course. Why not connect the two? They'll be thankful you did.

54 The Importance of Categorizing Contacts

> **"**
>
> Recognizing where people fit in the grand scheme of your ultimate network will keep you from jumping the gun and taking the wrong approach to building relationships.
>
> **"**

You can't push a marshmallow into a piggy bank. No matter how hard you try, it just won't squish through the slot.

Trying to push a general contact into the target market category before he is a qualified prospect will generate the same frustration for both of you. So will asking a general contact to send you a referral before trust has been established or a business relationship has been developed between the two of you.

Recognizing where people fit in the grand scheme of your ultimate network will keep you from jumping the gun and taking the wrong approach to building relationships. In the future, connectors are likely to become clients or they may send referrals to you, but establishing this comfort level and mutual trust takes time.

55 Following Up

Once you've categorized your contacts and have a good sense of the people you know, you'll need a game plan to take these relationships to the next level. Your 1, 2, 3 categorization system will determine with whom you need to connect and the best course of action to move those contacts to the next level.

TARGET MARKET CONTACTS AND FOLLOW-UP

A target contact has the highest priority in terms of follow-up. These are the people you've determined are ready to move into the sales process with you.

Recently, I attended a political convention where I met a gentleman who is a partner in an international accounting firm. The conversation naturally led to what I have been doing since the end of the political campaign. Using the 5-10-15 Communication approach (Refer to Chapter 48.), I explained that I had re-launched my company and was doing training and consulting on business networking.

By the end of my 15-second communication spot, he self-identified as wanting further information about my services for his firm's young accountant training program. I got his business card and that was the end of our business talk at the convention.

When I returned to my office, obviously he was a priority follow-up. Right away I sent him a personal note with a marketing package outlining the training workshops I could offer to his company. Weeks later I received a call from his Human Resources department to book a session.

This is an ideal case scenario for turning casual business card contacts into business relationships. I didn't have to "sell" my services; I just educated him on what services I offered. He did the "selling" inside his firm for me. The brief discussion (our entire conversation was no longer than five minutes) made this contact very easy to categorize as a target market. My appropriate course of action was very clear.

The firm had to hire someone for their training programs and now that I had connected with a senior level partner, I had an advantage over my competition. All I had to do was follow through, as promised, after the convention. Unfortunately, many professionals would fail to do this. If I had ignored his suggestion and not followed up, I wouldn't have been considered, let alone given the contract.

For the most part, this scenario reflects how I've built my entire company. It's also how I pursued donors during my career in the not-for-profit sector. I don't do cold calls and I don't try to sell my business services to people who don't want or need what I have to offer.

A straightforward approach to follow-up with contacts in your target market will earn you respect and a professional reputation. This is not the time to be wishy-washy or second guess yourself, your product or your services. You've already qualified the contacts as potential buyers so give them the opportunity to buy or use your services, not those of your competition.

When you move people into the sales process after an initial introduction, reference the reason you have identified them as a potential client.

For example, *"Hi Martha, just wanted to follow up from our conversation last night at the event. You mentioned you're looking for an accountant. As discussed, I am an accountant and would be pleased to meet with you to see if I can fill your needs. Here are some available dates: (insert dates). Let me know if any of those times work for you."*

Simple, short and to the point. There is no guess work or hidden agenda, but there is an excellent opportunity to develop a business relationship. Providing you presented a genuine, welcoming professional image when you met, Martha should respond to your message. She has already identified that she is looking for your services, so the easier you make it for her to hire you, the more likely she will be to do just that.

CONNECTORS AND FOLLOW-UP

Following up with Category 2 contacts known as "the connectors" is also a priority, but this re-connection takes a different tone. The purpose is to create relationships, not to sell your product or charge for your service.

Ideally, a reason to follow up is determined during your face-to-face encounter. Once you've already agreed to have coffee, lunch or a golf game, then the follow-up is easy. Contact the person within a reasonable amount of time to make arrangements for the meeting to happen. If you wait longer than two business days to follow up, your contact may forget what the two of you agreed to do.

The same time guideline applies if someone offered to connect you or give you advice. A common mistake people make is failing to follow through on generous offers made by general contacts and connectors.

A person who offers to introduce you to someone or let you pick his brain usually means it. If he didn't genuinely mean it, but you follow up anyway, he is technically on the hook to help you. Most likely, you will earn respect by calling him. This person now knows that you are someone who should be taken seriously and who takes others at their word.

> **Those who have earned significant success are usually genuinely happy to help others achieve the same.**

I introduced a good friend to a very successful businessman. At the time, my friend, although successful in his own right, was looking to change his career path to create a more fulfilling lifestyle. The businessman, who had made a similar transition years earlier, gave my buddy his card and offered to help. It was obvious he had a lot of relevant wisdom to share and was genuinely interested in sharing it. Unfortunately, my friend never took advantage of his offer.

Months later, the successful businessman and I ran into each other. He mentioned that my friend still hadn't called him. He then shared a story of another young professional to whom he made the same offer. Unlike my buddy, this fellow sent him an email later the same night asking to book a meeting.

Which contact do you think is on track to building a professional relationship with this businessman? Both are equally talented and credible men, but one followed up – the other one did not.

Those who have earned significant success are genuinely happy to help others achieve the same. Call it a pay-it-forward equivalent in the business world.

When a specific reason for follow-up has not been established, it may make sense to wait before making contact through a potential Connector. Experience will help you determine the best rate for reconnecting. When in doubt, take a step back and look at the situation from a long-term perspective rather than focusing on the immediate returns.

Was there enough of a mini-bond established between the two of you so that when you call, he will remember who you are and want to pick up the phone? If not, when will you likely see this person again? Running into him a second and third time will establish more familiarity and will allow the relationship to build at a natural pace. Patience and perseverance are key elements.

If you sit on a committee together, depending on the dynamics of the group, it may make sense to wait a few meetings before making plans to connect one-on-one. Likely, an issue will arise that requires the two of you to meet, giving you an opportunity to get to know each other better. Allowing an appropriate pace for a connection to grow will strengthen the foundation for a long-term, mutually beneficial business relationship.

There are people with whom I rarely spend one-on-one time, yet they are still valuable members of my network. They are considered valuable members of my network because I know who they are, what they do and what they have to offer and I like them, trust them and think they are competent and vice-versa.

Sending these people referrals or picking up the phone when I have a quick question does not require an "official" networking meeting.

GENERAL CONTACTS AND FOLLOW-UP

Following up with general contacts will take yet a different tone. Any communication with this group is about strengthening the connection in hopes of eventually moving them to the Connector or Target Market categories.

A common error that occurs is people follow up with casual General contacts as if they were Connector or Target Market contacts instead. It is unwise to send an email suggesting a business referral relationship after meeting someone briefly.

Here's an example of a follow-up email modelled after this detrimental, albeit far too common, approach.

"It was great to meet you last night. I am attaching my marketing materials. If you happen to know anyone who needs my services, I would appreciate any referrals you could send my way. Likewise, if I hear of anyone looking for an ...' insert profession here'... I will be happy to send them to you."

Really? Why would you be happy to do this? On what grounds are you basing the single greatest business compliment ever – the act of sending someone a referral?

> **It is unwise to send an email suggesting a business referral relationship after meeting someone briefly.**

Those who send and receive referrals know it happens naturally once a certain level of comfort and trust is established in relationships. Most importantly, on what grounds do you feel you have the right to ask this new acquaintance to refer you to others?

This technique reminds me of the relationship book titled, "I Love You, Nice to Meet You" by Lori Gottlieb and Kevin Bleyer. If you make such significant gestures to practical strangers, you will appear insincere and you won't be setting yourself up for success.

After meeting someone briefly, a personalized email that reflects the reality of your limited relationship but opens the door for future dialogue is more appealing. For example:

"It was great to meet you last night at the event. Hopefully, our paths will cross again. I'd like to get more involved in the community so if you hear of any other events you think may be worthwhile, by all means please let me know. By the way, if you run into our mutual friend, xx, please give her my best."

While the first email comes across as insincere, canned and pushy, the second offers a genuine, non-threatening attempt to keep in touch. It has a greater chance of making a long-term connection. At this point in the relationship, your email signature indicating what you do through your company name and potentially your tag line will suffice. The welcoming content of your email will help build the connection between the two of you, while your signature at the bottom of your e-mail will begin the education process as to what you do.

As you build your professional network, you will find a groove that works best for you. The key is to keep the process as natural as possible, matching your efforts with your personality.

You don't need to follow up with everyone you meet. Contacts in your General category usually don't require any immediate contact unless you are specifically hoping to move them into Category 2 or 3. However, take notice of those in your general contact list. Make a mental note to remember them the next time you connect.

You never know, perhaps the next time you run into each other, your general contact may introduce you to someone in his ultimate network who will become a Target Market contact for you.

56 Maintaining Relationships

Great relationships start with the basics. Get to know people, understand their needs and learn what makes them tick. A genuine interest in others will make you likeable, will generate trust and will create a foundation for future business opportunities and meaningful relationships.

As you expand your network and bring new associations into the fold, you'll want to ensure you maintain your current relationships. There are certain people whose relationships will be easier to sustain because you will interact with them on a regular basis. Among them are fellow committee members, key clients and good friends.

It's the people on the peripheral of your inner circle who require more deliberate attention. Find your own way to keep in touch with these people for non-business related purposes.

Often in networking people will only call when they need something. Treasured relationships are developed in between the crunch times. If every time you call a contact it's because you need something, the natural back and forth development of the bond is hindered. This reactive attitude towards networking creates relationships that are about supply and demand rather than meaningful connections.

Relationships will ebb and flow. There are times in the year when people are more active in the business community, whereas other times support a less intense pace.

> **"**
>
> **A reactive attitude towards networking creates relationships that are about supply and demand rather than meaningful connections.**
>
> **"**

For example, during the summer months professionals still work but there is a much less formal business environment as people take vacations and focus more on family. This is a perfect time to host a company's family picnic or invite people to participate in summer activities like golfing or boating.

Another strategy is to lunch every day with different people. Having lunch once a year with your Connectors is a great way to stay in touch. Throughout the year you will still interact at business functions or when pertinent issues arise, but planning some one-on-one time to catch up is enough to deepen the mini-bond. Depending on the relationship, it may be worthwhile to have your "annual" lunch more frequently, perhaps every six months, once a quarter or on a monthly basis.

One friend makes several Happy Birthday calls each day. He is known as the guy who will call you on your birthday. For something that takes him about 10 minutes a day, it's a gesture that is always appreciated and it gives him an excuse to make contact. Another friend calls people to wish them Happy Anniversary to mark their first lunch meeting together.

Staying abreast of who is in your network and what's happening in their lives is a great way to stay connected. When someone you know is mentioned in the media, send them the clipping with a congratulatory note.

This also applies to their family members. There is nothing more satisfying for parents than to see their children succeed. Recognizing their children's achievements is equally gratifying.

When you plan to attend an event, send the notice to contacts you would like to get to know better. Perhaps you can pull together a table for the function. It's a great opportunity to play host and introduce other people as well. Just because you send the notice does not mean you have to pay for the tickets. Simply ask them to call the hosting organization to purchase their own tickets, ensuring they mention they'd like to sit at your table. You can also mention the ticket price in your request. For example, "Tickets are $50 each, payable to the xxx Association." This implies that they are to pay their own way.

If an associate mentions a challenge they are having and a potential solution crosses your desk, feel free to send the information. When someone is looking for a job or information, introduce him to someone in your network who could potentially help.

57 Tapping into Your Network

It's one thing to know a lot of people; it's another thing to be able to tap into those resources. People who network well establish a professional environment that encourages networking and collaboration. By networking with others, they set the stage for others to network with them. They've learned how to maximize the give-and-take roles that naturally occur in relationships.

The first requirement to tap into your network is to have a network established. If people don't know who you are, what you do and what you have to offer, nor do they like you, trust you and think you are competent, you won't have a foundation on which to draw.

Build your network before you need it. It's never too early to start. Even if you're not looking for a job today, you never know what the future may bring. It's easier to request a donation from a contact with whom you've communicated for two years than from a person you've met once.

To tap into your network, you'll need to be clear about what you need and when you need it. Don't be shy about letting people know you are looking to grow your business, are open for new job opportunities or are hoping for their charitable support for a fundraiser you're volunteering to organize. When you are networking properly and professionally, people will want to help you and see you succeed.

> **People who network well establish a professional environment that encourages networking and collaboration.**

Give advance notice and plant seeds well ahead of when you need their help. For example, if you've joined a fundraising committee, when you are engaged in conversation with contacts, let them know what you're doing. A simple, *"I'm volunteering for XYZ charity. Looks like we've got some great events coming this fall. I will definitely keep you posted as details are available."*, will subtly give them notice to expect your call.

This approach will help you get past a "gatekeeper" when you do call, because technically you can say that he's expecting to hear from you. If you're developing strong enough relationships, you should not have to worry about being screened by assistants because the person you're calling will want to take your call. It won't happen right away, but eventually this will be the reality.

Most of the time, people who know you, like you and trust you will want to say yes and will go out of their way to make a request from you a reality. If they can't help, they will at least want to help you find someone who can and/or point you in the right direction.

When the first call you plan to make to a new contact is for a request, be sure you've established a mini-bond during your initial in-person introduction.

As well, set the expectation that you will call in hopes of getting them involved in a project. This up-front communication avoids any unnecessary surprises.

> **"**
>
> **When you have a need, before looking to the yellow pages, consider who's in your network first.**
>
> **"**

When you have a need, before looking to the yellow pages, consider who's in your network first. Who can help you? If you don't know, then who in your network would likely have a contact who could help you? Call him to ask for a recommendation. It gives you a chance to connect and it gives your contact a chance to send a referral to a person in his network.

Constantly ask yourself, "Whom can I connect with whom?"

Do people have problems that you can help solve? This is not an attempt at sainthood, but rather just a conscious effort to recognize challenges, identify needs and find solutions for others around you.

When you make an effort to do this, first ask the people you are connecting if they would like to be connected. This way you'll avoid over-stepping your boundaries by putting two people together when one or both are not interested in being connected.

The safest option is to simply give a referral. *"If you don't find anyone to solve your problem, it might be worthwhile to call so and so who does this. Feel free to let him know you got his name from me."*

There are formal and informal networking relationships. The bulk of your opportunities will be informal. These are the people in your network you may call from time to time, but there are no expectations attached to the association.

Formalized networking opportunities can be very advantageous to grow your business, provided each participant participates equally. Business clubs with the expectation to send each other referrals are great, but far too often only one or two people will send referrals, whereas everyone else takes them.

You don't need to be a member of a business club to benefit from formalized referral activities. Partnering with like-minded professionals who offer complementary services can create a lifetime of positive business benefits, but again, only if the relationship is mutually beneficial.

This kind of a referral partnership should only be entered into if you share similar values for client service and have the capabilities to deliver an acceptable quality of service. Developing this kind of a coveted relationship is not to be taken lightly. As discussed earlier, offering a referral is an enormous gesture of trust.

When tapping into your network, be aware that each person in your network has a natural threshold for what he can offer to your relationship. Calling in a favour can have a domino effect if the person has to call one of his trusted contacts to help you.

Many professionals damage relationships by not respecting the goodwill expense it takes to make special requests happen. People are happy to help, but it's an important consideration to decide when, and to what degree, you can cash in on your influence and the resources of people in your network.

"

Those who have more substantial, meaningful relationships will have more clout when it comes to making requests and drawing on the goodwill of their relationships. That also means, they'll likely be more guarded when it comes to making requests of people in their circles of influence.

Constantly ask yourself, "Whom can I connect with whom?"

"

A friend of mine went out of her way to arrange a private box at a premier sporting event for one of her associates. The fact that she could make it happen spoke to my friend's strong networking abilities. At the last minute, her associate decided she didn't want the box anymore. In relationship terms, it was a disaster. My friend lost her influence and her shot to pull in a once-in-a-lifetime opportunity for someone who whimsically decided she didn't feel like going to the event anymore.

To make matters worse, her associate didn't realize the magnitude of her actions. My friend maxed out her goodwill threshold with a contact and it will be a long time before she can ask for another favour from him.

To continually return to the same person to ask for favours can deplete your relationship quickly. When you make a call for a major request, be sure it's worth it. When you're going to go for it, go for the gold. Just recognize what each person's "gold" threshold is in relation to your association.

This concept is best explained when I reflect on my days as a professional fundraiser. My experience was that a relationship could get you in the door to make any request. It was up to you to seal the deal. Your success depended on how well you could judge what the appropriate donation request amount should be.

Asking for a $5,000 donation when a person was capable of $50,000 meant you left the opportunity for another $45,000 on the table. On the opposite end of the spectrum, if you went into the meeting requesting $50,000 when the donor's capacity to give was only $5,000, you would walk away with nothing because you asked for too much and made your potential donor feel uncomfortable.

> **"**
>
> **When you make a request, be sure it is realistic in terms of what the person can give and reflects the depth of your relationship.**
>
> **"**

Likewise, if you asked for $1,000 this month, but actually needed $2,000, you couldn't return to make an additional request from the same person the next month. However, if your initial request was for $2,000 over two months, you would arrive at the desired outcome.

My experience was primarily in annual fundraising and corporate sponsorships, so my philosophy was that I could ask potential donors to contribute once per year, provided I maintained the relationship in between.

Networking relationships work the same way. You only get one shot to call in a major favour. Until you replenish the goodwill in the relationship by returning the good deed, giving appropriate recognition or sending business referrals, it's tricky to go back and ask for more.

When you make a request, be sure it is realistic in terms of what the person can give and reflects the depth of your relationship. Follow through on the request and show appropriate appreciation.

58 Staying Visible

To maximize your networking efforts, you'll have to stay top-of-mind for your contacts. You may recall, one of the two key objectives for networking, as discussed in Chapter 4, is to ensure that when your contacts have a need, they will think to call or recommend you first.

Once networking momentum is developed, it's easy to get a false sense of security and drop off the scene. This is dangerous because it will give your competition the opportunity to swoop in and take your place.

To stay at the forefront of your contacts' minds, either you need to interact with them or they need to think about you. You can't be everywhere and talking with everyone so finding strategies to keep you fresh in their thoughts is imperative to leverage your networking efforts.

The "interacting with you" part of the equation is easy. It's just time consuming. It means staying visible by attending appropriate events and engaging in one-on-one networking activities. Every time you connect with a person, you re-establish yourself as a part of his network.

Keeping people thinking about you requires more creativity. When you can't be present, you still want the buzz about you to be there. This buzz, much like your reputation, is incredibly powerful when it is positive. Negative buzz can be equally powerful, but is detrimental.

There are several ways to raise your profile. The focus board that we will establish in the coming chapters will assist you in deciding where to target your efforts and how to align your activities with your long-term objectives. By figuring out who you want to know, it's easier to decide how to become visible. Are you looking to appeal to the masses or to a specific sector?

For example, if you sell men's clothing, becoming a columnist for a women's fashion magazine is not advantageous unless your marketing strategy is to appeal to women to buy your product for the men in their lives.

When I worked in the media, it was easy to stay visible. People could easily catch me on radio, on television or in the newspaper. This profile proved to be an asset for other projects I had on the go.

A full-blown media career is not necessary for you to reap the benefits from the power of the press. People are always looking for quality information to print. Submitting interesting and relevant columns to trade publications, local media and/or industry associations for their newsletters can garner you quality profile in the community and with your target market.

News sources often have a list of "experts" they call for quotes when breaking news occurs. Develop relationships with your local media and make yourself easily accessible so they will think to call you. Obviously you must have substance, not just style to keep these relationships alive and credible.

Volunteer to be a guest host for your local radio and television stations. You can go one step further and purchase air time to host your own radio show on AM Radio, community television or place an advertorial in the newspaper.

Earned media is arguably the most powerful way to build profile and add credibility to your reputation.

I remember talking with a group of people at an event. They were all so excited that their associate had been featured in a two-page spread in the newspaper's business section and asked me if I saw it. I didn't have the heart to tell them: I actually wrote the article.

It just goes to prove, being the one sharing the story is not as important or as powerful as being the person who is the story.

If media doesn't appeal to you or won't help you achieve your objectives, there are plenty of other opportunities to create profile.

At the bare minimum, every professional should take a leadership role in a volunteer capacity. Whether it's for a business association, a recreational activity or a charitable cause, adding something of significance to your resumé will help you establish yourself and expand your network.

> **"**
>
> **At the bare minimum, every professional should take a leadership role in a volunteer capacity.**
>
> **"**

It's more effective to be actively involved in one or two activities than to spread yourself too thin by joining multiple associations. Use your focus board (Refer to Chapter 59) to establish the best places for you to invest your time.

Hosting annual company events is a great way to stay visible and raise your profile, provided you have the budget to do so.

An additional possibility is sponsoring events and looking for logo and name placement opportunities at functions that attract your target market. Each time a person notices your logo, especially when it is attached to a worthwhile cause, it will add to your goodwill bank account.

An effective way to stay top-of-mind is to develop a mass email blaster or newsletter for your clients and contacts. These can be valuable tools, provided you follow some simple guidelines as best laid out by Michael Hughes, a fellow networking consultant and president of *Networking for Results*.

I met Michael through this stay-in-touch technique when I launched my company. A local lawyer had been receiving his weekly e-tip for years, so when I told him about my plans to start my company, he forwarded me a copy of Michael's e-tip. Michael bases his e-tip on three simple criteria:

1 Value-based

2 Short

3 Permission-based

If you choose to set up an e-tip, e-zine, e-newsletter, or do something in print, these are valuable rules to follow.

59 Finding Your Focus

When I wrote the column for the newspaper, I had a rule: no more than seven events in one day. You may be thinking, "Yeah right, no more than seven events in one year." My recommendation is to meet somewhere at a comfortable place in the middle.

The point is that there is always something happening. There is always somewhere you could be and always another cause to support. To manage the possibilities, make filling your calendar a proactive activity, not a reactive one. Instead of responding to invitations solely based on your availability and whether or not you "feel" like attending, add strategy to your networking efforts to avoid the "mud-on-the-wall" approach mentioned earlier.

There are four steps that will combine to create your personal focus board. This will make it easy for you to choose the right events to attend and to focus your networking efforts.

1 **DEFINE YOUR PURPOSE**

2 **DETERMINE YOUR TARGET MARKET**

3 **IDENTIFY YOUR INTERESTS**

4 **COMMIT YOUR RESOURCES**

STEP 1: DEFINE YOUR PURPOSE

From a business perspective, what are you hoping to achieve by building your professional network? Several networking benefits are listed below. Rate each benefit #1 to 12 in order of importance to you.

_____ Raise company profile

_____ Raise personal profile

_____ Increase sales

_____ Increase referrals

_____ Gain access to specific target markets

_____ Find investors

_____ Achieve personal fulfillment

_____ Develop professionally

_____ Recruit new employees

_____ Help shape your industry

_____ Plan for succession (i.e. transferring current business relationships to someone else in your company so you can retire)

_____ Set other goals: _____

STEP 2: DETERMINE YOUR TARGET MARKET

Who are you hoping to meet? The best way to determine your target market is to write down your top five clients or connectors. Consider who they are, what makes them tick and what specific qualities put them at the top of your list.

Does their line of work or income affect their need of your product or service? Are there certain personality traits that draw you to these people? What do they do for work? What do they do for play? How do they spend their time? What causes do they support?

The more you know about with whom you want to connect for work and/or play, the easier it will be to identify where you should go and with whom you should spend your time. It will also help you identify people who can move into your Connector and/or Target Market categories.

List your top five clients then list their characteristics.

TOP FIVE CLIENTS

_____

_____

_____

_____

_____

THEIR CHARACTERISTICS

_____

_____

_____

_____

_____

STEP 3: IDENTIFY YOUR INTERESTS

Getting involved in activities that make you miserable will make it difficult for you to connect because you'll be unhappy at the event. No matter how hard you try to mask your true feelings, people around you will sense your mood and will, consciously or subconsciously, avoid you.

Conversely, focusing your efforts on activities that align with your interests and passions can ignite enthusiasm into your networking efforts.

A client talked about all the golf tournaments she was going to enter that summer. I was confused because I thought she disliked golf. Turns out, she couldn't stand the sport, but thought she had to golf to build her network. I wondered why.

Another client loathed working on dinner committees. She had organized her fair share of fundraising dinners and because she was good at it, she was routinely asked to assist. Much to her chagrin, she always felt compelled to say yes. That changed once we generated her focus board and she learned how to say no. (Refer to Chapter 50)

Make these clear distinctions so you won't get caught doing what you dislike. It doesn't mean you always get to do what you love, but for the most part you can avoid the angst of participating in activities that don't fit with your personality.

> *The list below can help you do this. Decide if an activity makes you happy, sad or neutral. Then, you can build your entire networking strategy avoiding experiences that make you unhappy while filling your calendar with activities that make you happy or, at the very least, keep you neutral. Check one emotion for each activity.*

LIST OF ACTIVITIES

☺ ☺ ☹ Conventions	☺ ☺ ☹ Lunching
☺ ☺ ☹ Conferences	☺ ☺ ☹ Hosting dinner parties
☺ ☺ ☹ Politics	☺ ☺ ☹ Board work
☺ ☺ ☹ Dinner events	☺ ☺ ☹ Committee work
☺ ☺ ☹ Galas	☺ ☺ ☹ Event organization
☺ ☺ ☹ Charity events	☺ ☺ ☹ Professional development
☺ ☺ ☹ Award ceremonies	☺ ☺ ☹ Dining clubs
☺ ☺ ☹ Playing individual sports	☺ ☺ ☹ Associations
☺ ☺ ☹ Concerts	☺ ☺ ☹ Service clubs
☺ ☺ ☹ Theatre	☺ ☺ ☹ Book clubs
☺ ☺ ☹ Listening to speakers	☺ ☺ ☹ Cocktail parties/mixers
☺ ☺ ☹ Coaching	☺ ☺ ☹ Golf
☺ ☺ ☹ Family activities	☺ ☺ ☹ Golf tournaments
☺ ☺ ☹ Working out	☺ ☺ ☹ Business groups
☺ ☺ ☹ Charity runs	☺ ☺ ☹ Issues-based organizations
☺ ☺ ☹ Watching sports	☺ ☺ ☹ Playing team sports

STEP 4: COMMIT YOUR RESOURCES

To build your network you will have to participate in activities that connect you with people. This requires time and money. How much time and money you need to spend will depend on your goals, objectives, resources and timeline. It will also depend on your personal and work commitments and your bank account.

To spend time with people who have money to invest or donate, you will have to go where people with money go – which will likely require more funding. To meet small start-up business owners who have less disposable income will require fewer financial resources.

Set an initial annual budget and review it after a few months. You may need to redirect resources from your advertising or direct marketing budget to accommodate your new networking objectives.

How much time are you willing to invest to build your ultimate network? No doubt you are busy, but if your goal is to build the ultimate network, you will have to set aside time to network.

A reasonable and effective pace is to commit to one or two business events and three one-on-one networking activities each week. There are times in the year when everything seems to happen all at once. Yet, there are other months when it feels like you're living in a ghost town. Make this cycle work in your favour. Slower times of the year are perfect times to connect one-on-one. You can have fewer one-on-one encounters when the event circuit is particularly heavy, as you will no doubt see contacts at events.

As you commit resources, determine if there are certain times that you simply can't or won't focus on business network development. For example, Tuesday nights you play hockey and Sundays are family days. Write these boundaries on your focus board on Page 200.

STEP 5: CREATING YOUR FOCUS BOARD

> *Fill in the blanks on your focus board using the information from steps 1 to 4. In the future, check to be sure your networking activities fit your focus board.*
>
> *To download your own focus board, visit www.elevatebiz.ca*

...The Ultimate Network

✓ Step 1. PURPOSE

1 _____

2 _____

3 _____

4 _____

✓ Step 2. TARGET MARKET

1 _____

2 _____

3 _____

4 _____

✓ Step 3. INTERESTS

Likes

☺ _____

☺ _____

☺ _____

☺ _____

☺ _____

☺ _____

Dislikes

☹ _____

☹ _____

☹ _____

☹ _____

☹ _____

☹ _____

✓ Step 4. RESOURCES & COMMITMENTS

Time

Number of business networking events per week _____

Number of business associations _____

Number of one-on-one activities per week _____

Times not available: _____

Budget

$ _____ monthly budget (activities)

$ _____ annual dues (clubs/associations)

$ _____ entertaining budget (meals/tickets)

STEP 6: CHECK YOUR ACTIVITIES

From now on, when an invitation crosses your desk, simply refer to your focus board and ask yourself:

- Would attending this function get me any closer to my goals and aspirations?
- Would my attendance there put me in front of my target market or people who are connected to them?
- Is this event one I would enjoy?
- Does this event match my time and money resources?

Going through this checklist each time you consider participating in a networking activity will help you focus your time, manage your finances and make good decisions.

An event that does not meet at least three of the criteria on your focus board should not be considered as a proactive business networking opportunity.

> *To begin your proactive approach, write down all of your current business networking activities. Put each one through the focus board test. Which ones fit? Which ones don't fit?*

CURRENT NETWORKING ACTIVITIES
FOCUS BOARD FIT

	PURPOSE	TARGET	INTERESTS	RESOURCES
_____	❑	❑	❑	❑
_____	❑	❑	❑	❑
_____	❑	❑	❑	❑

	PURPOSE	TARGET	INTERESTS	RESOURCES
_____	❑	❑	❑	❑
_____	❑	❑	❑	❑
_____	❑	❑	❑	❑

Enjoyable activities that do not fit your focus board should be considered social activities, not business networking activities. Yes, there are always hidden opportunities at the ball park because you don't know who'll be attending, but we're being proactive and trying to put you in a winning situation.

Staying in your comfort zone and keeping busy with activities that don't fit your focus board is not a good time investment from a business perspective. Building a social network and a business network are two different priorities.

If your priority is to increase sales, finding activities that attract potential clients for your company makes good business sense. Spending all your time at industry association meetings to build relationships with your competition doesn't.

If professional development is a top priority, then industry-related meetings that offer training and industry insight are definitely worthwhile.

An investment advisor, who spent the bulk of her networking time with one organization, wondered why she wasn't seeing a business return after years of building relationships within the group. When asked about her target market, it was clear that she wanted to attract individuals who met a certain investment threshold. We discovered that none of the members of the organization she belonged to had that kind of money available to invest. There was the reason for her disconnection.

The fundraiser who spends all her time meeting with other fundraisers and thinks she is busy networking is kidding herself. She may be having fun, but it's unlikely she'll find big donors in the mix.

You can't expect to turn contacts into business relationships if you're constantly surrounding yourself with people who don't qualify as potential fits for your product or service.

60 Filling Your Calendar

Now that you have a focus board, you can be proactive when developing your business networking plan. Research available opportunities for networking so you know where you want and need to be.

Look at your city's networking circuit. What's happening? What are the big events of the year? Where do the movers and shakers and your target market spend their time?

It may take you a year to get into the loop. You can't expect to be included on an invitation list for events you've never attended or expressed an interest in attending. As you hear about events that you missed, keep a log and plan to attend next time they occur.

The easiest way to find the best places to go is to ask members of your network the two vital questions we covered earlier.

- Where should I go?
- Whom should I meet?

Ask people you meet in one-on-one settings these questions and they will give you more than enough options to fill your calendar. Keep in mind, these contacts don't have access to your focus board, so don't feel you have to go everywhere that is suggested. Remember, check your focus board before you commit to any events or activities.

> *Make a list of the top 20 business events in your city each year and build your calendar around those activities.*

Building the Ultimate Network

TOP 20 NETWORKING
OPPORTUNITIES IN THE CITY

	MUST ATTEND	SHOULD ATTEND	WON'T ATTEND
1	❑	❑	❑
2	❑	❑	❑
3	❑	❑	❑
4	❑	❑	❑
5	❑	❑	❑
6	❑	❑	❑
7	❑	❑	❑
8	❑	❑	❑
9	❑	❑	❑
10	❑	❑	❑
11	❑	❑	❑
12	❑	❑	❑
13	❑	❑	❑
14	❑	❑	❑
15	❑	❑	❑

	MUST ATTEND	SHOULD ATTEND	WON'T ATTEND
16 _____	❏	❏	❏
17 _____	❏	❏	❏
18 _____	❏	❏	❏
19 _____	❏	❏	❏
20 _____	❏	❏	❏

Next, look for obvious networking opportunities. Read the business section in the newspaper. Read trade journals and look for events and conferences that will attract your target market. Is there an industry association where you can get involved? Are there charities that interest you and meet your focus board criteria? Are there causes that you're passionate about that would attract like-minded people?

Don't stop finding networking opportunities until your calendar reflects your goal of one to two formalized business activities and three one-on-one meetings per week. Refer to your list of Connectors. With whom do you want to meet first? Are there people you should reconnect with right away? Once you've blocked off time for networking meetings, call your contacts and fill your calendar.

Yes, there will be days when you won't feel like networking or when you're too busy to go out for lunch, but I suspect there are days when you don't feel like going to work and yet you still do. You have to go to work; it's how you earn your living.

Now that you're learning how to network properly and professionally, networking will directly contribute to the ease in which you can achieve success. Before long, connecting with others will become second nature and will be a high priority in your calendar.

61 Analyzing the Options

Networking opportunities are everywhere.

They are on the subway, in your office elevator or on the street. Just leaving your house each day makes you eligible for great chance encounters. Everyone has at least one random introduction success story. Keep your head up when you're in public, be open to meeting new people and be aware of potential opportunities.

Since this book is designed to help you develop a proactive networking approach for long-term results, we will leave the chance encounters to chance and focus on the formalized options that can help you build your network.

The more involved you become, the more you will notice an increase in invitations and requests for support. Your focus board will allow you to decide which activities are best for you.

As you develop your professional network, you will find what works for you and what activities you truly enjoy. Below are some perspectives on various networking opportunities to help you make decisions about how to best invest your time and money.

BREAKFAST MEETINGS give you an early start to your day. They get your networking out of the way so you don't have to interrupt your work-day. Breakfast is usually reasonably priced so if your budget is tight, this is a sensible option.

LUNCH MEETINGS are a great way to break up your day. Find your favourite lunching hot spots so you know what to expect in terms of food, service and price. Lunch meetings are a solid opportunity for casual one-on-one discussions that deepen your professional connections. Also, you will likely run into other professionals while lunching. Official business discussions tend to happen after the main meal. It is difficult to eat and look at business papers at the same time.

Be prepared to pick up the cheque. It can get a little pricey unless you're meeting with people who have expense accounts. "Taking turns" is very acceptable and more professional than splitting the bill unless your lunch is with a close friend or associate with whom you eat regularly. If a person insists on paying, it is appropriate to accept someone else's generosity. A thank-you note after the fact adds a nice touch.

COFFEE MEETINGS are quick, easy, informal and inexpensive. Have coffee meetings in your office to maximize your time or find a comfortable coffee shop close to your work.

CHARITY FUNCTIONS are a superb place to meet people while supporting a worthwhile cause. Complete your pre-event homework before you go so you have an idea of who will be there. Who is sponsoring the event? Who volunteers for the charity?

Watch your budget. Costs at these events can add up quickly, especially when charities encourage you to spend money at the function in addition to the ticket price. Senior level management and executives are often in the room so it's a worthwhile investment to attend if they are your target market.

INDUSTRY-RELATED ASSOCIATIONS provide many rewarding opportunities to shape the future of your industry. You can learn from your peers and network effectively. Associations give you a chance for professional development and opportunities to sink your teeth into projects, all of which can earn you a reputation as a go-to person. Through your involvement in the association, you can earn recognition as a leader in your industry. Just be sure your potential customers see that as well, not just your peers and competition.

COMMITTEE WORK is a very hands-on approach that will allow you to make a positive impact on a project and raise your profile. There are always more than enough opportunities around for good volunteers. Use these committee meetings to establish your reputation as someone who delivers. Strive to under-promise and over-deliver.

SERVING ON BOARDS is an appealing way to shine in the community. Your involvement on a board would provide an excellent opportunity to do some rewarding work and add something impressive to your resumé. Before making the commitment (minimum two years, but likely six) ensure you understand all the expectations. What are the time and financial commitments? Are you responsible for raising funds? If so, are you comfortable doing that?

SPECIAL INTEREST GROUPS attract like-minded people. People united for a cause such as the environment, politics, or religion are likely to form deep connections because they already have core beliefs in common. Joining the local environmental group, even though it may not specifically serve your target market, can lead to expanded circles of influence.

A friend was hired by a law firm. His boss was particularly excited about his extracurricular activities as he saw huge potential for him to bring referrals to the firm. For years he'd taken leadership roles in both the political realm and the Pride community. Much to his surprise, all of the business the young lawyer has brought to the firm has been a direct result of the networks developed through his involvement with these two causes.

BUSINESS NETWORKING GROUPS and clubs operate with the expectation that everyone is there to connect for business. Before joining such a group, attend a couple of meetings as a guest. Do you feel comfortable? What's the tone of the group? Is your competition a member or would you be the only representative from your industry? Do members do business together? What are the expectations of membership? Are the membership fees, if applicable, appropriate for your budget?

Can't find the right networking club? Why not start your own? Some of the most productive networking groups originated thanks to like-minded people coming together with the specific intention to build relationships and send each other referrals. Each month the group meets and each member has to report on his interaction with other members.

Caution: Business groups and associations can become comfort zones. It's easy to go back to meetings week after week before realizing you're in a networking rut. Staying with a group when you're not enjoying it, especially if it doesn't fit your focus board or isn't leading to business relationships, is not a wise business investment for you. Don't be afraid to change your choice of activities every couple of years.

CONVENTIONS AND TRADE SHOWS by their very nature, attract people with similar interests. They are a great place to learn about competition, resources and innovations. Pre-event homework is imperative to make these events worthwhile, especially since they often require travel and a time commitment of up to several days. Make a list of whom you want to meet.

For annual events, call or email contacts in advance to let them know you'll be there and that you look forward to seeing them. If there is specific business to discuss, let them know in advance that you would like to meet for a coffee sometime over the course of the trade show or event.

Visit the hospitality suites and mingle to meet and reconnect with contacts. Avoid spending the whole convention in your comfort zone talking with your work colleagues.

To really get your company noticed, consider sponsoring a portion of the convention, providing refreshments during the breaks or hosting your own hospitality suite. As an individual, taking a leadership role on the organizing committee can get you noticed and make it easier to meet conference attendees.

PRIVATE GOLF GAMES require significant time and financial investment (depending on where you play), but can be worthwhile provided you pick your partners well and you are able to keep your composure for extended periods of time. Golf games are great when you are looking to establish or deepen a professional relationship with a specific person.

A lot can be said about a man's character by how he lets a little white golf ball affect his day. If you have a tendency to kick the ball from the rough onto the fairway using a "foot wedge", throw your club or refuse to count ALL your putts, then avoid taking business contacts on the golf course.

Remember, you want people to like you, trust you and think you are competent. Emotional golfers or those who routinely and conveniently forget to follow the hard and fast rules of golf lose credibility on the course, which, in turn, detracts from their perceived credibility in the boardroom.

Business talk is usually kept to a minimum, but the relationship built over a fun, relaxing golf game can lead to closing deals. If you do choose to golf, be sure to learn the rules of golf etiquette. Here are just a few must-knows:

- Count all your shots.
- *Do not talk* while someone is on the tee box or taking a shot.
- Don't use your cell phone on the course.
- Keep pace of play with your golf mates and the foursome in front of you.
- Wear the appropriate regulation golf attire.

GOLF TOURNAMENTS can create bonds, but primarily with the three others in your foursome. Shower quickly after the game and stick around for dinner so you can maximize time to connect with others at the tournament. Don't spend all the time before and after your round with your same foursome. You'll have plenty of time to connect with them during the game and at the dinner.

Unless it's a staff bonding day, sharing a cart with a colleague is not a wise investment of time or money. Try to share a cart with a potential client or new contact. Be prepared to lose an entire day out of the office to attend a tourney.

Golf tournaments rarely help your golf swing; the best ball format can make it frustrating for those who take the game too seriously.

The rules of the game still need to be respected, even though it's a fun day on the course. Drinking alcohol should be kept to a minimum.

↗ Section 4 Summary

- Be proactive and strategic about your networking efforts.

- Ask contacts the vital questions – Where should I go?
  Whom should I meet?

- Use an electronic filing system for tracking contacts.

- Develop a user-friendly system to categorize your contacts so
  you can identify proper pace for follow-up and next steps for
  relationship management.

- Follow through with your commitments.

- Once relationships are built, make a concerted effort to maintain
  and nurture them.

- Find ways to remain visible to your network. Don't fall off the
  radar screen, thus giving your competition the chance to create
  bonds with your contacts.

- Check potential networking events against your Focus Board.
  Activities that don't fit your criteria are not considered priority
  areas for building your professional network.

- Proactively fill your calendar with opportunities to connect with
  people. Analyze the options available and make good strategic
  decisions about where to invest your resources.

62 Becoming the Ultimate Connector— Making Your Mark!

The gentleman who sparked my passion for networking (remember the lawyer who took me to my first committee meeting) is considered by many to be the quintessential networker or, as I like to call him, the ultimate connector.

He takes great pleasure in helping others build their business networks. He has a habit of taking young professionals under his wing, showing them the way and then freeing them to make life happen with the people they meet. I have wondered what my life would be like today if my mentor hadn't reached out to me when I was 25.

I have thanked him on various occasions for changing my life, but he's reluctant to accept my praise. He doesn't feel that it is necessary to thank him because he believes that helping others is just the right thing for him to do. There are plenty of his "recruits" who attribute the start of their networks to him. In the truest sense of the word, he is a "connector".

The only thing he asks in return is that we go on to become successful contributing members of the community. At 85 years old, he still works every day as a senior partner in his law firm. I'm sure his networking efforts earned business for the firm, but being or becoming a client was never a stipulation of his generosity to others.

The loyalty he and his wife have generated, thanks to their incredible commitment to the community and the people in it, is amazing. Their desire to connect people is admirable and the benefits they've received go far beyond just building a successful career. Their kind efforts have contributed to a quality of life and personal fulfillment that relatively few get to realize.

The same thing can be said about the person who asked me to attend the political reception on that critical Saturday morning. Since then we've become the best of friends and she and her husband continue to be posi-

> **"**
>
> **Your path to the ultimate network begins with you becoming an ultimate connector.**
>
> **"**

tive forces in my life.

Imagine being that person for someone else – a true connector. Imagine changing another's day for the better or altering another's life thanks to an introduction you made. When you consider it a priority to bring people together, the possibilities are endless. These good deeds will inevitably boomerang to reward you when you least expect it.

Looking back on my life, there are several people who fall into this "ultimate connector" category. These are the people who genuinely want others to prosper. They go out of their way to make others feel comfortable and to help them find success. Their lives are spent looking beyond themselves and inevitably, success and fulfillment follow.

Your path to the ultimate network begins with you becoming an ultimate connector. Start by noticing what people in your network need, even just the little things that will make such a profound impact. Bringing people together to work for a common goal can have rewards galore for all involved.

Having a generous spirit with others and taking your eyes off your own personal needs may not have immediate rewards, but these actions will contribute to an unsurpassed quality of life.

As a result, you will earn a reputation as someone who networks well and you will be differentiated from those who don't. When you surround yourself with great people, great things happen – that's how the universe works.

It is my belief that the most satisfying aspect of networking is becoming part of someone else's success story. ■

END NOTES

1. Prince, Russ Alan and Lewis Schiff. *Middle-Class Millionaire: The Rise of the New Rich and How They Are Changing America.* USA: A Currency Book published by Doubleday, 2008.

2. Encarta Dictionary: English (North America)

3. Neumeier, Marty. *Zag: The Number One Strategy of High-Performance Brands.* Berkeley: Peachpit Press, 2005

Recommended Reading

Over the last several years, I've read countless books, all of which have helped shape who I am today. I've found that each book offers its own tidbit of information that usually fits exactly what I need at that specific time in my life.

As I peruse my bookshelves, I recall that the books below made a profound impact on my professional life. Not surprisingly, many of these are best sellers, so I'm not alone in my opinion. If you're looking to continue to grow, might I recommend reading these books if you have not already done so.

1 *How to Win Friends and Influence People* by Dale Carnegie

This was the first self-improvement book I read and arguably, it had the most impact. Written years ago, the principles still apply today.

2 *First Things First* by Steven Covey, A. Roger Merrill and Rebecca R. Merrill

This book was instrumental in teaching me how to focus my efforts on priorities rather than letting over-loaded to-do lists control my life.

3 *The Imperfect Board Member: Discovering the Seven Disciplines of Governance Excellence* by Jim Brown

This easy-to-read book is essential for anyone who serves on boards of directors. It clearly conveys the proper roles and responsibilities of members and outlines effective organizational flow.

4 *Good to Great: Why Some Companies Make the Leap and Others Don't* by Jim Collins

This book is an excellent resource that teaches the difference between companies that have success and those that fall short.

5 *Now, Discover Your Strengths* by Marcus Buckingham and Donald O. Clifton

Before I launched my company in 2006, I couldn't quite pinpoint where I wanted to go next with my career. Learning my five key personality traits and seeing how they could translate into business helped me envision how I could make those intangibles work for me.

6 *Mirror Mirror on the Wall Am I the Most Valued of Them All?* by Leo Pusateri

Understanding your value and differentiating yourself from your competition can be difficult, but necessary if you want to succeed. In my estimation, Leo Pusateri is the number one resource to teach you how to determine your value and articulate it well.

7 *Think BIG and Kick Ass in Business and Life* by Donald Trump and Bill Zanker

The fact that a Trump book would hit my list of favourites would surprise some who know me, but it does. Reading this book was the defining moment for me when I had to re-establish my life's goals and re-launch my company after the political campaign. It opened my eyes to the possibilities in business and motivated me to get out there and make it happen.